THE TEACHER AND CHRISTIAN BELIEF

THE TEACHER AND CHRISTIAN BELIEF

BY

NINIAN SMART

JAMES CLARKE & CO. LTD.
LONDON

First Published 1966

© JAMES CLARKE & CO. LTD.

For
Peregrine

MADE AND PRINTED IN GREAT BRITAIN BY
THE GARDEN CITY PRESS LIMITED
LETCHWORTH, HERTFORDSHIRE

CONTENTS

5

PREFACE

THE aim of this book is to discuss certain key issues about Christian belief which are relevant to those engaged in the teaching of religion. The assumption lying behind this aim is that teaching is not likely to be effective unless we have evolved some point of view about what we are teaching. The object here is not to impose such a point of view. The whole spirit of this book is antipathetic to this idea. Rather the evolution of a point of view can put us in a position effectively to engage in the dialogue with those who themselves, in the process of learning, are reaching towards a point of view. Since it is also a central concept in this book that Christian belief must be understood in relation to contemporary knowledge and experience, the attempt is made to show how the dialectic between revelation and the contemporary world holds the promise of yielding insights into both. Though my theological and philosophical arguments and conclusions may not be correct or acceptable, at least the discussions here presented can serve as a starting point for the reader in the evolution of his own conclusions. To repeat: there is no idea here of imposing a point of view.

Given that Christian belief has to be seen in its contemporary setting, and yet at the same time rooted in its historical origins, the first main part of the discussion concerns the nature of the Biblical revelation and the best manner of approach to it. Since the idea of revelation presupposes that of a transcendent Being, lying as it were "behind" the world we see, the discussion moves on to an analysis of

this idea. This soon brings us up against the common attitude, here called "scientism", which would want to rule out
an "invisible" world, on the ground that it is not open to
scientific investigation. This sets the stage for an account of
the relations between science and religion. This is connected
to an exposition of the doctrine of Creation. It is argued
that this doctrine can be supported, though not proved, on
grounds which arise from our reflection about the cosmos.
The doctrine is also one which can serve to illuminate
human creativity, in the arts, sciences and in morality.

This discussion introduces an attempt to analyse the
human situation, including human freedom, here regarded
as a social, not just an individual, phenomenon. This analysis extends to the "darker" side—to attempt to understand
the nature of sin and estrangement. Here we have to achieve
a synthesis between what we experience, both in society and
in ourselves, and the traditional, poetical account of the Fall
of Adam. The human condition of estrangement has, of
course, according to Christian belief, a cure—through the
work of Christ. This act of salvation is seen in relation to
the creation of the "new society"—the Kingdom.

The next phase of the argument concerns the relation of
Christianity to other religions. An interpretation is given to
the idea that God reveals himself in those faiths. The problem of other religions raises questions about religious experience, and there is a consideration of the arguments
about its validity.

The earlier discussion of freedom, sin and salvation
stressed the social dimension of the human situation. Another aspect of this is considered in the posing of questions
about the manner in which Christian attitudes can illuminate
moral, social and political aims and institutions. This
approach is further elaborated through an attempt to see
the nature and relevance of the Trinity doctrine.

Finally, the foregoing theological and philosophical discussions are argued to yield conclusions, in the shape of

guiding principles, which are intimately relevant to the whole process of religious education.

These, then, are the main topics treated here. Naturally, much of importance is missed out and much is treated too briefly. But the aim has been at least to elaborate a coherent point of view which exhibits the results of the dialectic between Christian faith and contemporary knowledge.

I have not gone in for footnotes, nor are there many references to influential theologians and philosophers. I have preferred to let the argument run its course without too many distracting excursions into the views which are held by different individuals and groups. But those who are stimulated by the discussion can take off in all sorts of directions of their own, and to help them I have appended a bibliography related to the various points made in the text.

Since the assumption of this book is that clarification of ideas is important (though I fear the ideas of this book have not reached an ideal state in this respect), I have preferred to leave on one side the discussion of the views of Existentialist theologians (with the exception of a brief consideration of Bultmann)—theologians who have been enormously influential in our day, at least among their fellow-theologians. They no doubt have quite a lot to tell us, and they figure in the bibliography. But they are not always suitable stepping-stones towards a clarification of our ideas.

The pattern of argument in the book has been greatly determined by the idea, mentioned above, that there must be a dialectic between our intellectual and moral world on the one hand and the Biblical revelation on the other. The arguments thus are not, at least from one side, simply neutral nor simply humanistic. But it is hoped that they exhibit an openness of approach towards the sceptic and the humanist. This is essential in any context. It is especially important if we are to begin to answer questions. And what can teaching do if it cannot engage in this particular dialogue?

Parts of the book may seem a bit "theoretical". I only hope that those who think so will read on. What is theoretical also sometimes turns out to be practical.

Finally, let me add one point. The intellectual side of religion is not to be treated with disrespect. It is no easy thing to teach religion, for many reasons. Commitment and enthusiasm are not enough. The increasing number of excellent people teaching in this area, at all levels of our educational system, is a heartening tribute to the seriousness with which we are beginning to take this intellectual dimension of religion.

What would St Peter, a simple fisherman (so some say), think of all this? Well, first, he was no fool. And second, we live in a different world.

NINIAN SMART

Tremezzo
August 1965

CHAPTER ONE

THE PROBLEM OF BELIEF

RELIGIOUS knowledge is taught in our schools. This already presents a nest of problems. What knowledge? What religion? And who teaches?

Some of those who teach are anti-religious; others are uncommitted; others again are Christians. Our schools also contain Jews; and will increasingly contain Sikhs, Muslims, Hindus and Buddhists. For ours is a plural society. How does one satisfactorily arrange for the teaching of one religion in a plural society?

But then what are people supposed to teach? The phrase "the teaching of religion" is ambiguous. Does it mean that youngsters should be influenced to become Christians? Are they somehow to be given faith? This is one meaning of "the teaching of religion". Or is it that they are taught the facts *about* religion? Is the teaching of religion simply the teaching of the history of religion? Here is a second sense of the phrase.

But things are not so simple. For one thing, people do not agree on what the history is. Again, there are wider questions—such as those about the relation between religious belief and a scientific outlook—which are not to be resolved by appeal to the facts, but which are philosophical in nature. Religion is controversial.

It is also like poetry in having different layers of meaning. The superficial sense of religious language conceals depths which require understanding and insight. This is why simultaneously it can appear childish and profound.

It is why it attracts both contempt and love. It is why religious understanding involves growth. If we do not recognise this poetical side of religion, we shall miss much, and even the teaching of facts *about* religion will be sterile.

It follows that if the teaching of religion (however we interpret this phrase) is to be meaningful, it must involve a sympathetic attitude in the teacher. Understanding needs sympathy.

But this can sound sinister. It sounds like an old Christian ploy. It sounds like saying: "To understand it, you have to believe it; and if you do not believe it, you cannot be rational in your unbelief, for how can you reject what you do not understand?" It also sounds like a recommendation that a Trojan horse be smuggled into our schools. Those who conscientiously feel that Christianity is false, or outmoded, or corrupt, or dangerous, or foolish, may interpret the slogan that understanding needs sympathy to imply that only committed Christians are qualified to teach religion. Does this not entrench bias?

Certainly there are not wanting Christians who would argue that religious knowledge must be taught by the committed Christian. There are Christians who regard religious knowledge as a rightful part of the religious establishment in this country. There are Christians who appear fanatical to the outsider, and who import such fanaticism into their teaching. It is no wonder that suspicion and recrimination are not far away when the slogan that understanding requires sympathy is voiced.

The anti-religious suspicion and the Christian sensitivity are alike unrealistic. They both rest on outworn assumptions. They both belong to a period that ought to be over. They both do damage to ourselves and to our children. They both are productive of the very resentment and difficulty they seek to annul.

Let us look again at the matter, first from the side of humanism, and second from the side of Christian belief.

The humanist is concerned with the welfare of mankind,

with the spiritual and material enrichment of men. But what is welfare? It is not just orange-juice, wages and medicines. It is not just houses and clean air. These things are necessary to human welfare, because without them men would suffer and die. But men seek a happiness that is not merely negative. Without penicillin, men would perish of bronchitis and pneumonia: but otherwise we have but little interest in penicillin for its own sake. No, our happiness is found in the promotion of the things we love. The gardener finds satisfaction in his peonies; the cricketer in his cover-drive; the singer in his song; the mathematician in his theorems; the husband in his wife; the child in his toys; the young and old in their friends. These are basically useless joys. They are not, like useful things, means to an end; they are ends in themselves. Welfare, then, means, among other things, the promotion of what men value and the production of what gives them joy and inspiration.

If humanism means the promotion of human welfare, it also involves respect for individual men. What men find good—this is what they should, if possible, obtain. It can be no part of humanist ideology to say: "What you value is just rubbish." It is true that sometimes human values are distorted. Men often go for trivial rather than more illuminating satisfactions. They gain little joys, but miss the bigger ones. But in general, the humanist has to respect the individual's joys. If he is to give men a deeper vision of the good than that which they sometimes have, it must be by persuasion and argument, by example and education.

The humanist's attitude to religion must be moulded by these considerations. It is undeniable that many men find value in their faith; that many men look on their welfare as tied up with the contemplation and worship of God; that many men see communion with God as an end in itself. It is only a crass humanism which would dismiss this dimension of human experience and aspiration. The humanist may deny the premises upon which the religious man acts; but he cannot deny that religious joys and ideals are pursued by men. If he thinks that men here pursue illusory goals, his attitude should be this—to persuade by argument and example.

Moreover, whatever faults and inconsistencies the humanist may find in religious belief, he can hardly remain insensitive to the positive worth of some religious phenomena. Religious art, architecture and music are not nothing; Christian love has sometimes been exemplified; the lives of Christ and the Buddha are not without significance for those who do not share a religious outlook.

It follows that a sensitive humanism will involve a certain sympathy for religion, because of the part it has played in the pursuit of human welfare. It also follows that the humanist must engage in argument and persuasion: he must be in dialogue with that which he rejects.

From the point of view of the teacher, this surely must mean a sympathetic portrayal of religion. Of course the blemishes in Christian history need not be overlooked. But equally it is necessary to extract from Judeo-Christian history the things which have moved men, the positive values which men have found there, the beauties and challenges which have given Christianity its dynamic.

From the side of Christianity, too, there is no need to take a fanatical line. Why force religion down young people's throats? The duty of the teacher, surely, is to relate the Bible and Christian belief to the experiences and needs of those who are taught. This must in the end mean dealing with the questions and doubts which young people bring to Christianity from a plural environment. It must in the end mean entering into dialogue with a semi-scepticism. It is not just the young person brought up in a non-religious home who may express such a scepticism: the Christian too has a perpetual dialogue with himself and with his faith. This is part of the growth of understanding. It is illusory to suppose that doubt lies all on the side of the "outsider".

For these reasons, the Christian teacher, if he is to be effective in this area, must be sympathetic to doubt. He must be sensitive to criticisms of religion. He must see religion in relation to the social and intellectual realities of our own day. He must not be so fanatically committed that he is jumpy and blind. Christian commitment can be a hindrance as well as a help to teaching. This is why it is outmoded and absurd to adopt traditional partisan attitudes to the teaching of religious knowledge. Both the humanist and the Christian must essentially, in their teaching, be in dialogue. The good teacher is not the Christian one or the humanist one. The good teacher is the open one.

But then some teachers are neither Christians nor humanists. Some are just indifferent to religion. What of them? Two solutions to the problem are possible. The first is quite simple. Let them not teach religious knowledge. The second is less simple. Let them teach it, and if they remain indifferent to religion, then ask them questions. A person who can find nothing fascinating or challenging in what he teaches must be suffering from some blindness.

The moral of the preceding discussion is this: that there is no need for anyone to be frightened about the teaching of religious knowledge. Or rather, no one need be frightened of it if it is *well* taught. For good teaching is hostile to hostility, it is closed to a closed mentality, it is prejudiced against prejudice, it is against narrowness, it is opposed to indifference, it is in dialogue with the real world from which young people spring. The problem, after all, is not the problem of what the teacher believes; it is not *this* problem of belief. It is the problem of insight.

It is therefore important that the teacher should be reflective. It is easier to teach when one has, through reflection, gained a clearer understanding of one's position. Hence the aim of this book will be, not so much to show what ought to be taught to ten-year-olds and what to the Sixth Form, as to engage in an extended reflection upon Christian belief. The use of this will be indirect, but it may not be the less important for that.

In any event, the questions of children are usually relevant. The child's questions foreshadow and express problems which recur at a more sophisticated level. And teenage religious questions are very often those which the teacher once asked himself, but forgot to answer. It is then that the shoe pinches. Clarity about one's own position, then, is vital.

A problem, of course, arises, when we try to estimate our reactions to Christian belief. For there are beliefs and beliefs. Christians are not intellectually united. Some, for instance, are very liberal in their understanding of doctrine and in their attitude to the Bible. Others have a more monolithic position. Those who believe in the detailed infallibility of the Scriptures are far removed from the Bishop of Woolwich. Those who accept the infallibility of the Pope are far removed from the Quakers. It is illusory to think that there is a single set of propositions which can express Christian belief.

Again, the reasons why some reject Christianity can vary as widely. Those who are disillusioned with the Church reject it for one reason; those who identify Christianity with fundamentalism reject it for another. And so on.

In view, however, of the structure of religious education in this country, and the system of Agreed Syllabuses, the main issue will be the way in which we treat the Bible. Here above all a reflective attitude will contribute to the whole approach to teaching and to the selection of material. It is thus important to consider this issue at the outset. Now it is unlikely that the arguments which I shall use will be accepted by everyone. I shall be outlining a possible position. But it would be a mistake to think that the arguments, because not universally acceptable, are without point. The keynote of the present discussion is that attitudes should be *reflective*, not that they should be stereotyped. The open discussion of the issues will surely contribute to reflectiveness.

CHAPTER TWO

CHRISTIAN BELIEF AND THE BIBLE

IT is very difficult to appreciate the Bible properly. Though it is an ancient collection of documents, it is read out in Church as though it is a contemporary work. It is bound up with history, and yet it is often treated as timeless. It bears the stamp of human writing and editing, and yet it is also identified with the word of God. It is quoted in snippets, as though everything in it is of equal value; and yet in terms of religious significance it is uneven. Our attitudes to the Bible are overlaid by the practices of the Churches. It is hard, then, to see it in its own time and place.

Also, we are used to speaking of the Bible, as though it was always a fixed entity—as though it was always obvious that these books, and only these books, which compose it ought to be included in the sacred collection. We treat the Bible, in short, unhistorically. We fail to understand what it meant when it was written.

Yet this is a paradox. The Jewish and Christian faiths have always been in an important sense rooted in history. That is to say, they have involved an interpretation of historical events. They importantly concern, not timeless myths, but dated events. This is what is meant by saying that Christianity is an historical religion. All religions have had their rise in history (this is indeed a shallow tautology); but not all religions have tied themselves so closely to an interpretation of the meaning of the historical events through which they have had their rise. For Christianity, the life of Jesus is central. It was his acts, so the Christian

17

believes, rather than his teachings which brought to men their salvation. Thus Christian faith centres on historical events. It is surely paradoxical to treat Christian revelation timelessly and unhistorically.

Fortunately, we live at a time when a new perspective on the Biblical writings has been provided by more than a century of modern historical research. Though the conclusions of scholars are sometimes mutually contradictory; though much speculation has entered into those conclusions; and though there remains a lot to be done; nevertheless, anyone remotely acquainted with this work will appreciate the degree to which it has restored an historical reality to the Christian faith. Modern historical scholarship, though it has introduced scepticism about the veracity of some portions of the Bible, has also made us see Christian origins in a fresh and more realistic light.

All this has occurred in spite of opposition. Churchmen were often afraid of historical speculation. The authority of the Bible seemed to be undermined, at a time when it was being treated essentially as one would treat any other ancient document. Orthodoxy seemed to be threatened. For the Catholic Church, the danger of "modernism" was that it had implications about the Church's authority in matters of faith and morals. For the Protestant Churches, it was disturbing that the supreme source of doctrinal authority was being called into question. It is not surprising that many Christians did not altogether welcome the new look in Biblical scholarship. The resulting conflicts have led to the formulation of a number of basic positions about the Bible and about revelation.

These basic positions can be crudely stated as follows. They are four in number, and they arise from differing views about Biblical authority and the relation between revelation and human knowledge.

By and large, it is possible either to accept or to reject the basic approach of historical scholarship. If one accepts it, then one has to reject the literal infallibility of the Bible.

What then becomes of revelation? The Bible, up to a point, itself supplies an answer. Essentially, it is what the Bible is *about* which is revelation. It is the Word of God, namely Christ, that is revelation, not the words of the Bible. It is God's self-unveiling in history, not the propositions of the Bible, that is what revelation essentially consists in. Thus we can formulate the first position as follows: the Bible is a fallible record of God's self-revelation in history. But as we shall see, this position itself can bifurcate into two, in accordance with differing ideas about the relation between the rest of human knowledge and revelation.

If one rejects the basic findings of modern historical scholarship, and treats the Bible as a fully inspired and infallible document, there is no special need to take the "nonpropositional" view of revelation outlined above, though it is quite consistent to hold that essentially revelation consists in God's concrete historical acts and that the testimony to these, as contained in the propositions of the Bible, is fully inspired by God and so inerrant. The view which rejects the basic findings of modern scholarship is commonly called "fundamentalism", but those who hold it tend to prefer the lengthy title "conservative evangelicalism". Unfortunately, controversies have tended to overlay and distort the meanings of the labels used. It is therefore convenient to invent some new terms for the purposes of classification.

To this end, I propose to label the first position "inductivism" and the second position "deductivism". According to the first, one must find out what the historical and divine events were like by investigation of the Biblical material, by sifting it, by methodical enquiry. According to the second position, one can deduce God's revelation from the Bible, because the latter is infallible.

It is worth while briefly to recapitulate the arguments used for these two positions, and the respective advantages and disadvantages which they possess. In favour of inductivism there are a number of obvious and weighty considerations. First, traditional deductivists interpreted the Bible to mean that the creation was a relatively short time ago. Such a position is refuted by the findings of geology and astronomy and biology. In a number of other ways, traditional deductivist interpretations of the Bible have proved fallacious. Second, though the writers of the Bible were by no means intending to write history in the modern manner, a crucial part of the message concerned historical events. It seems common sense to try to investigate such historical claims by modern methods. These imply an inductivist approach. Third, the thought-forms of Biblical writers (their "three-decker" picture of the cosmos, their belief in demons, etc.) clearly belong to a particular historical epoch. Inductivism has the promise of trying to sift out the true import of the Biblical message and testimony from the accidental trappings of the cultural environment of the Biblical writers. Fourth, the notion of verbal inspiration is hard to understand (as though St Paul, in dashing off a letter to Corinth, miraculously got everything—but everything—right).

On the other hand, the deductivists can make the following claims. First, if we begin questioning Biblical authority we shall know nothing for certain. Would God have left us so much at sea? Second, some inductivists have been too sceptical about Biblical historicity. Third, the Church has taken a generally deductivist line in the past. Fourth, Jesus himself quoted the Torah as though he too were a deductivist.

The disadvantages of inductivism are that historical fashions change, and that the erosion of Biblical authority may allow alien and unchristian ideas entrance into theology. The disadvantages of deductivism are, however, more severe. First, deductivism is continually liable to be in conflict with modern knowledge, and it seems that if deductivism is the correct interpretation of Christianity, Christianity must be false. Second, deductivism cannot answer the detailed questions about the Biblical narrative which semi-sceptics are inclined to ask. Consequently, it is educationally disastrous. Third, it is notorious that deductivists have interpreted the Bible in grossly differing senses. For the Southern Baptist in the United States, the Bible justifies segregation. For the teetotaller it justifies abstention (despite Jesus' first reported miracle). For the Catholic it justifies papal claims. For the Protestant it does not. Would God have left us so much at sea?—having to rely on the interpretation of an infallible Bible?

The first and second of these disadvantages are of crucial importance. For the adherence by many of the more zealous Christians to deductivism has given the impression to many atheists and agnostics that deductivism is the essential Christian position. Atheists are often deductivists upside down. They reject Jonah in the whale's belly, and Noah, and the demons, and so they reject Christianity. It is an ironical and even amusing situation. It is ironical because the atheist often rejects Christianity for precisely the reasons that inductivist Christians reject deductivism.

Because deductivism is committed to the details about Jonah and Jericho and so forth, it cannot seriously allow historical questioning. Did such things really happen, the child (who is father of the man) may ask? The Bible says so, is the reply. But what sort of a reply is this? It cuts off the real questions by the imposition of a total system of belief. There is no need to add that this cannot make for good teaching. Because a rigid deductivism is so educationally disastrous, there is perhaps no need to consider it further here, except to note that its modern manifestations are understandable in an age of religious crisis.

It is understandable because it stops questions. It represents an intelligible reaction to sophisticated scepticism. It solves intellectual problems by withdrawing the intellect from faith. It produces a kind of curate's egghead—hard-boiled in parts. It is new, because it is a reaction to modern knowledge, but it claims to be traditional. It produces a certain sort of good works. It is fervid and evangelical. But it would hardly work in schools, even if it flourishes oddly in universities.

Apart from the distinction between what I have called deductivism and inductivism, there is another polarity to consider. Generally speaking, Christians have taken two views about the relation between revelation and human knowledge. For some, human knowledge can supplement revelation. Thus St Thomas Aquinas formulated the classical Catholic position when he argued that some truths could be known about God through the exercise of natural human reason. Thus it is possible to distinguish between natural and revealed theology. Any attempt to reinterpret Christian belief in terms of contemporary knowledge of the world must involve some recognition of the validity of human reasoning and observation as a means of discovering something about God; it must thus involve some kind of natural theology. It may be that the distinction between natural and revealed theology has been too sharply drawn. But some such notion is involved in all attempts to co-ordinate religious and secular insights. We may call the thesis that natural theology is possible the "liberal" view.

The "revelationist" view on the other hand is the view that man on his own can know nothing of God. Just as salvation comes from God alone, so the saving knowledge of God comes from him alone. God's revelation is an utter challenge to the values and presuppositions of mankind. Karl Barth is the most eminent contemporary theologian to express such a revelationist position. For him, man's reason is fallen: thus there can be no natural theology. God's revelation comes as it were vertically from above.

The liberal and the revelationist views can be combined with those of deductivism and inductivism. This makes four basic positions. We can hold a liberal inductivist view (like Temple and Bultmann); a revelationist inductivist view (like Barth); a liberal deductivism (like Roman Catholics—though this analysis needs qualification, as we shall see); or a revelationist deductivism (like the Conservative Evangelicals).

The polarity between liberalism and revelationism will in

part determine the way in which we approach the teaching of the Bible. The revelationist view implies that we can learn nothing of God outside of his historical self-revelation. This means that we begin with the Biblical material and use it to challenge and illuminate the intellectual and social realities of the contemporary world. The liberal view implies, on the other hand, that things outside the Bible can prepare the way for the acceptance and appreciation of the Gospel. Educationally, there are advantages in both approaches.

The liberal approach can elicit the questions and problems as they arise for young people, and can serve to show that tentative answers to them can be confirmed in the revelation detectable behind the Biblical narratives. For example, the existence of the cosmos seems to call for explanation. That it is created and sustained by a God is one hypothesis. This hypothesis points in the direction of the Biblical revelation.

On the other hand, the revelationist approach stresses the challenging nature of Christ's acts and words. It stresses the way in which something new and unpredictable irrupted into human history. By its firm determination to begin with the historical revelation in Israel and in Christ, revelationism can impart a dynamism to the teaching of the historical narratives. We shall, however, observe that there are a number of intellectual disadvantages to a rigidly revelationist approach.

It is important on general grounds to clarify one's position, so that one knows in what category it falls, as between the four views distinguished above. But it is probably more important to grasp the exciting prospects opened up by our new historical perspective on the Bible. These are not simply to be equated with the fact that we can reconstruct more accurately the events about which the Biblical narraives speak and that we can understand better the processes of writing and editing which gave birth to this remarkable collection of documents. More importantly, we can begin to enter into the thought-forms and motives of those who wrote. For what has not been sufficiently clear to expositors of the Bible in the past is the way in which different strands of religious thinking have been woven together in the documents. Despite the marked emphasis on history found in the Bible, it is fallacious to think that the whole Bible was composed as an historical record in the modern sense.

For example, the accounts of the creation and of the Fall found in *Genesis*, though they are edited in such a way that they become continuous with the history of Israel, were born in a milieu in which a mythological expression of religious ideas was natural. Adam is not just an individual; he is the prototype of mankind. Through the story of his fall, the writers expressed what was also to them a present fact: an estrangement between God and man, through man's tendency to be destructive and disobedient to the will of God. The story of Adam has a relation to other myths in the Ancient Near East, but it is here given a unique shape in relation to the strong monotheism of the writer.

Now the fact is that we do not write that way today. We do not think in such mythological terms. Or if we have our myths they are of a very different stamp. It is thus impossible to read *Genesis* with understanding as though it is a contemporary document. We have to ask ourselves: "What was the type of literature to which the accounts of the creation and of the Fall belong? What was the writer intending in writing the way he did?" It is a distortion of the material to think that the writers of these accounts were attempting to write history in the way in which we understand it.

Thus most of the disputes about the literal truth of this early part of *Genesis* are beside the point. They involve treating the material as though it is on a par with Darwin's *Origin of Species*. It is like supposing that a poem and a text-book can collide.

The moral is that our new historical perspective can liberate us from a wooden and mechanical interpretation of the Bible. It can make us see the essential variety in the material. It can lead us to ask serious, rather than trivial, questions. A recognition of the fact that different parts of the Bible belong to different literary *genres* is also, as it happens, a means whereby deductivism can be powerfully modified. Thus a number of modern Catholic scholars, who hold a generally deductivist position, nevertheless reject the idea of a uniformly literalist interpretation of the Bible. This position can be described as "modified deductivism".

But it might be objected to the new historical perspective that it involves too radical a break with the past. Since Christians have for so long treated the Bible in a rather unhistorical manner, and since they have not consciously distinguished between what counts as literal history and what is poetical mythology, the new perspective seems to be a renunciation of past orthodoxies. This superficial impression is, however, mistaken, for a number of reasons. First, the power of a mythological account is not necessarily diminished by the fact that it is treated rather literally. At the subconscious level, the message of the myth can get across. Consider the parallel with parables, where a literally expressed story is known to have a deeper meaning. Likewise, the deeper levels of meaning in a mythological story can still function despite the literalism of the hearer. Secondly, there has been a long tradition in the Church of allegorical interpretation, going back to the early Fathers: this was in effect a partial attempt to supplement literalism with a spiritual and religious interpretation of outward events. Thirdly, Christianity has, virtually throughout its history, been in dialogue with its cultural and intellectual environment. The new historical perspective only represents a further extension of this process.

Nevertheless, the claims of the new perspective must not be exaggerated. Though it can help us to see that some questions have in the past been wrongly posed (for instance, the question of a clash between biology and the story of the creation of Adam), we are not thereby exempted from solving real problems about the relation between the Biblical tradition and modern knowledge. It is only that these problems are transmuted into a new key. For instance, though we can see the story of the creation of the cosmos as essentially a poetical and mythological expression of the dependence of the world on God, there still remains the problem of how this doctrine of dependence fits in with the attitudes of scientific cosmology. This is an issue which we shall be turning to in Chapter Three. Again, the Bible sometimes presents a highly anthropomorphic picture of God (he walks in a garden, for instance); yet at other times it strongly emphasises God's transcendence and difference from the created order. We need, in order to deal with this problem, to evolve a view of the nature of God which will convey both his personal nature, as expressed in anthropomorphic myth, and his otherness, as expressed too so powerfully in the Biblical insistence on the mysteriousness of God.

The essence of these problems is this: the Bible often speaks in images. We do not wish to take these images in a straightforward and literal way. We understand that they point to something beyond themselves. But we have to express this something. We have to be able to put into words what it is that the poetry is "getting at". This is not to say that such a "translation" exhausts the power of the images. It may well be that beyond what we can say there is something unstatable. Nevertheless, in order to extract from the poetry a conception of what it signifies, we must make the attempt to frame in intelligible language a doctrine of God. In brief, the Biblical images, by pointing beyond themselves, demand that there shall be doctrines.

This has, of course, been commonly recognised in the Church. The framing of a conception of God has been a protection against literalist anthropomorphism. The process, however, has its dangers. There is the peril, for instance, that the poetry may be lost; there is the danger that the doctrine may become too abstract; there is the danger that a metaphysical God will no longer correspond to the personal object of faith and worship; there is the danger that the God of the philosophers will not be the God of Abraham. But the opposite perils are equally great. There is the peril that a literalist God will be too puny to be a serious object of affection and awe; there is the danger that the anthropomorphic God will be an immoral one (as though God's wrath is really petulance, not an expression of his mystery); there is the danger that an anthropomorphic God will become an inhabitant of the cosmos, not its creator and sustainer; there is the danger that the anthropomorphic God will be incredible. The atheist who rejects the Bible because he takes it in a simply anthropomorphic sense is quite right to reject it; it is only that he has not asked himself some deeper questions of interpretation. He is of course excused by the way many Christians talk, for they too seem to fall into a like error (save that the significance of the myths may operate at an unconscious level).

It happens that the issue of anthropomorphism has recently made much public stir, mainly through the wide dissemination of *Honest to God*. The Bishop of Woolwich's book is in part an attack on crudely anthropomorphic ideas of God. It is thus worthwhile to consider in general what we mean by speaking of God's transcendence. This may supply a corrective to anthropomorphism, and clarify our ideas on the direction in which the Biblical images point.

It is fundamental to the monotheistic faith so slowly evolved in Israel that the whole world depends upon God. This does not, of course, preclude God's particular activity at certain points of time and space. But it means that in some sense God is operative everywhere. All this was expressed in terms of heaven and earth, as though God resides above the firmament and yet controls and creates all that goes on below. But the logic of the creation narrative is that the whole cosmos depends on God's creative power. He is "beyond" the cosmos.

We, of course, see the cosmos in a richer way today, because of the incredible discoveries of modern astronomy.

Ours is a huge, perhaps infinite, cosmos. Immense galaxies recede indefinitely into the light years. The earth and the solar system are less than a pimple on the face of this huge universe. This is a very different picture from that of the Biblical writers. Nevertheless, the principle of what they were saying applies equally to the immense cosmos of modern knowledge. The principle is simply that of the dependence of the cosmos, for its existence and processes, on the power of God.

This in turn entails that God is not part of the cosmos. He is not an inhabitant of it. He does not occupy a place beyond the sun or below Jupiter. He does not hide in another galaxy. He may manifest himself to particular people. He may seem to walk in the garden. He may become incarnate in Christ. But he is not an occupant of any particular place or time. He is, so to say, "outside space".

But this is a paradox. If I say that someone is outside the room I mean that he occupies a bit of space different from the space which the room occupies. "Outside" is thus itself a spatial concept. How then can one be outside space? Does it mean that God occupies a bit of space different from the space which consists in space? This is contradictory and ridiculous. Of course we do not take "outside" literally. It is an analogy. (The Bishop of Woolwich tried another—"deep down", but of course God is not literally deep down, in my bowels or in a coal mine.)

But what analogy are we using? Before we answer this, let us briefly consider the role of analogies. An analogy is a non-literal use of language, like "He saw the point of the joke I told him". Naturally, one does not literally see the point of a joke, but we know what is being said. We continually in all sorts of contexts use analogies. Without them we would be cramped in communication and warped in understanding. The development of science itself depends to a great degree on the evolution of analogies (radio-waves are not sea-waves—they are not literally waves; genetic inheritance is not literally inheritance; an electric current is not literally a current). There is no reason to be suspicious of analogies. On the contrary. And yet we sometimes feel uneasy, as though the literal is the best way of speaking. Perhaps some of this unease comes from the mistaken idea that analogies are "mere metaphors", replaceable extravagances of speech. If anyone believes this, let him try rewriting science and music-criticism in a way which employs only the literal. There is, then, no reason why we should insist on literalness in religion, while abandoning it so largely in other areas of human thought and discourse.

But what do we mean by saying that God is outside space, or if you like outside the cosmos? One thing we mean, no doubt, is that God is not spatial. It does not make sense to say that he is ten or a million feet long. But then it does not make sense to say that a number is ten or a million feet long. We mean, then, something more as well. For one thing, we mean that God is not identical with the cosmos, but yet stands in a certain relationship to it. This relationship is that of continuous creativity: God is continuously creating and sustaining the cosmos. Without God, the cosmos would not exist, and would not continue to exist.

So far we may sum up the notion of God's transcendence as involving that God is non-spatial and that he is continuously creative of the cosmos. But more: we feel that God is somehow "behind" the things we see. It is as though he is hidden by the cosmos, save where he chooses to manifest himself through particular events and experiences. This mysterious hiddenness connects up with the ideas of holiness and of revelation. God, it is stressed in the Biblical material, is all-holy. In ritual terms, the holy object is that which is screened from profane gaze, or to be manifested only on solemn occasions. By extension, the whole world is seen as a screen. Only on God's initiative is this screen or veil removed, when the Divine Being is unveiled, revealed. This aspect of God's "beyondness" can be summed up as his mysteriousness. (Of course, God is not like a mundane mystery, like the mystery of who killed the victim in a murder story: religion is not to be identified with a list of unsolved problems in science or what have you—though sometimes religious apologists appeal to these, thus generating the so-called "God of the gaps".)

So far, then, God's transcendence means: non-spatiality, creativity and mysterious holiness. By implication from the second, it also means that God is operatively present everywhere: that we can see him "behind" the sprouting of the tree and the revolutions of the planets. Being operatively present everywhere, he is everywhere accessible to prayer and adoration.

It will be seen from such an outline of the idea of God's transcendence that there is no need to think of God as "up there" or "out there". If he sometimes seems distant this is the distance of alienation and estrangement, not the distance of rocket-ships. Equally, there is no need just to think of God as "deep down", as though he exists in the depths of human relationships alone. There is a danger in confining God's activity to his relations to men, to his operation as Love. The danger is that the trees and the planets as objects of God's creative power will be forgotten.

This point bears on a certain difficulty in revelationism, as opposed to what we have called liberalism. It is this. It is not unfashionable to interpret revelationism in terms of relationships. Thus a number of theologians attempt to see the Biblical message as having essentially to do with the relationship between God and his people. The creation itself is seen in terms of the covenant with Israel. Now there is something to be said for this interpretation. The Biblical writers, as we have said, connected the creation narrative intimately to the history of God's people. But, of course, there are other strands of thought in the Bible. The essential monotheism of the material implies a wider perspective on the creation. The danger, then, of translating revelation into terms of personal encounter and interchange between God and man is this: God's essential function becomes his being a person who has dealings with man. This "existentialist" revelationism is compatible with the idea of a finite God. It is compatible with the idea of a God who has dealings with the earth but not with the galaxies. It is compatible with the idea of a finite God. And a finite God is not compatible with the God of Christianity—with the God of the Old and New Testaments.

Consequently, there is a danger—though no more than a danger—that revelationism may produce an anthropomorphic and finite God. Yet this is paradoxical: for a liberal approach, though it is more likely to stress God's activity throughout the natural world, can itself be so influenced by secular thinking that it, in a certain sense, may make God in man's image. The paradox is this: that two conflicting approaches may equally encourage anthropomorphism. Nevertheless, it is probable that liberalism is more alive to the danger of anthropomorphism—partly because it is less self-assured, and therefore more self-critical; and partly because it is less inclined towards a deductivism which may treat the cruder language of the Bible as being on a par with its deeper and more self-effacing imagery.

God's transcendence, then, can be understood as meaning that the cosmos is dependent on a holy Being. As we shall see, there remain problems about this conception. Nevertheless, it serves to point to certain important lessons. First, because God is operative everywhere (though he is himself, as we have seen, "outside space")—operative everywhere because the continuing processes of the cosmos are dependent on his will—there is no need to think of God as distantly "up there". The conception of transcendence presented here (which is in essence that of traditional Christian theologians) can stimulate a "practice of the presence of God". It is thus important for the teacher to emphasise that, however anthropomorphic the Biblical God may appear at times, this God after all is essentially one who is present to us all the time. It is important that his sustaining power should not be thought of as a kind of remote control.

He is to be found in the trees, in the paving-stones, in the chimneys, in the finger-nails, as well as in the heavens. This is the main Christian belief about God, and a God of the gaps and of battles long ago is not adequate to this noble and exciting conception.

Second, the doctrine of God's transcendence can be used in a dialectical relationship to the stories and parables of the Bible. These parables and stories themselves are a vivid way of presenting God's particular activity and his personal nature. They stimulate insights through the use of concrete events and images. They serve to express God's self-manifestation to a chosen people. Without them, the Christian picture of God would never have got painted. Without them, there would be no recognition of God's word. Without them, there would have been no valuation of the historical dimension of God's activity. All this is true: but at the same time, God's particular manifestations need to be complemented by a recognition of his general activity. The chosen people must be seen against the background of a chosen universe. The Incarnation occurs in polarity with the creative Fatherhood of God. The temporal and spatial "interventions" of God must be seen in conjunction with God's heavenly life "outside" space and time.

In short, it must be recognised that revelation is not just revelation of revelation: it is the revelation of a Being who stretches beyond that aspect of his activity which is revealed. Unless this is seen, there is the perpetual danger that the God of the Bible will be trivialised and demoralised.

This discussion of transcendence has arisen out of a consideration of the kind of insight that the new historical perspective on the Biblical material can provide. It has arisen thus because the new historical perspective can allow us to distinguish between poetry, or mythology, and the literal use of language. It can stimulate a sensitivity to the main point towards which a particular writer was working.

But there is another aspect of the new historical perspective which is important for the appreciation of the Bible; and it is an aspect that has been touched upon already. It is this. The more we discover about the composition of the Biblical material the more aware we are of the order in which the material was brought into being and the order in which it was edited. It is, for instance, illusory to suppose that the first part of the Bible (the *Genesis* narrative) is the oldest; just as the Gospels are later than some of the other parts of the New Testament. This awareness of dating itself can stimulate a greater and deeper appreciation of the historical embedding of revelation. It can renew our insight into the uneven historical processes whereby the Jewish people came to accept monotheism. It can remind us that —for the Christian, as for the Jew—God's "intervention" in history is indeed in history. It can help to clothe religious realities in the flesh and blood of living, temporal men. It can dispel that "timeless" and uncritical view of the Bible which makes that collection seem boring and irrelevant.

Of course, it might be thought absurd to say that by dating the Biblical revelation—by placing it firmly in the past—we are thereby making it relevant. After all, what have we, in the twentieth century, to do with ancient events? Ancient history is all right for those who have the taste for it, but . . .

But the truth is that a supposedly historical revelation which is treated timelessly degenerates into a mere fable. It must be seen as having to do with real men and women. The story of Napoleon is for this reason more relevant than the story of King Arthur. Admittedly, it is sometimes difficult to enter into the past; it is often hard to get people to make the imaginative effort needed to treat the past as both past (and so not like the present) and present (and so not just a dead past). History is hard. There is no denying all this. But difficulty is different from irrelevance. It is better to be hard and relevant than to be easy and irrelevant. Thus the historical perspective represents an important challenge.

From the Christian point of view, all this links up intimately with the Incarnation. If it be true that God was in
Christ: that God walked the earth in the figure of Jesus;
that Jesus was God's central revelation to men—if this be
true, then it is no good neglecting the historical facts about
Jesus. It is no good seeing Jesus as a timeless figure. It is
useless treating him as though he lived today (even though in
a transcendental sense, Christ lives today). God became incarnate at a particular place and time—as a Palestinian Jew
under the Roman Empire, tall, swarthy, bearded, perhaps;
speaking a certain language; eating his food in a certain
way; replete with a stock of ideas drawn from his own
culture; having a certain religion. However startling and
original Jesus' teachings and actions were, it is obviously
important to appreciate them in their time and place. Many
of the absurd and unrealistic ideas of Jesus have sprung
from a lack of this historical perspective—as though he was
omniscient in a literal sense (and so knew all about Relativity Theory?—if so, he could have saved us some trouble
by declaring his encyclopedic knowledge), as though his
ethical teachings can simply be transposed without trouble
to a different type of society, as though he knew about
Aquinas and yet resolutely confined himself to parables
rather than metaphysics, as though the cross was really like
the crucifixes which may aid our piety, as though his beard
was a silkier version of that sported by King George V. In
short, the accentuation of the historical approach can rid
us of incredibility and sentimentality. We can begin to ask
what the man was really like. We can begin to smell his
sweat. God is not well represented in plaster.

Of course, the very particularity of the Christian revelation—its very historicity, its being tied to the Jews and
Jesus—represents a difficulty for many folk. It is not just a
matter of "How odd of God to choose the Jews"; more
importantly, it is a matter of the seeming exclusiveness of
Christianity. God reveals himself there and then, but what
about the everywhere and the everywhen? What about

India, China and Africa? What about modern England? Why does not God reveal himself in Wigan and Henley and Bolton, not just in Galilee and Jericho and Jerusalem?

Later, we shall discuss these questions in more detail. Suffice it to say at the moment that what is in question here is not so much the defensibility of the Christian revelation as its nature. What we must first be clear about is the latter. Questions then of its truth will arise. And it is essential to an understanding of why the Biblical material was put together and regarded as authoritative by the early Church to bear in mind the historical anchorage of Christian teaching.

Consequently, the new historical perspective can bring an exciting recovery of the meaning of these ancient events. This is a main reason why inductivism (however it may conflict with certain religious interests) is educationally fruitful.

Though, as we have seen, an understanding of the variety of Biblical material can remove some of the cruder conflicts between what we suppose to be a modern scientific attitude and what we suppose to be the Biblical affirmations, the suspicion may still remain that religious belief is somehow at odds with modern knowledge. This suspicion remains an obstacle to the sympathetic treatment of the Biblical material. For this and other reasons, it is convenient here to turn to a more extensive treatment of this topic. Is there a conflict between science and religion? Can men in a scientific and technological age genuinely see the world in the manner indicated by the Bible?

CHAPTER THREE

SCIENCE AND THE LIMITS OF RELIGION

THE prestige of science, through its intellectual and techno-logical successes, and the obscurantism of certain religious apologists have inevitably given rise to the impression that somehow a scientific world-picture will triumph over a reli-gious one. The impression is that religion is out of date. The impression is that for "modern man" the old categories must disappear.

There is no denying that many people in a modern society think in these terms. Their attitudes may not always be expressed in a sophisticated way, but in essence they centre on the affirmation that there are no facts which science cannot explore: there is, that is, no region of human knowledge lying somehow "beyond" the limits of science. Coupled with this attitude (which we may dub "scientism" —to adapt a term used by Karl Popper) is the hope that the modern technological revolution will bring immense blessings on mankind, provided only that men can live in reasonable peace.

Such scientism, however crudely and incoherently it may be expressed by the educationally under-developed mem-bers of society, is by no means confined to sophisticated folk. Though it is essentially a philosophical position it is not held only by professional philosophers. Though it is not uncommon among university graduates, it can also be detected easily enough in the secondary modern school.

The modern empiricism of Bertrand Russell and A. J. Ayer has, indeed, as one of its main roots the desire to bring philosophy closer to the scientific revolution which has proved so powerfully fruitful. Though most contemporary British philosophers would reject the brash Logical Positivism of Ayer's *Language, Truth and Logic* (even Ayer himself), there is no doubt that empiricism remains deeply influential. A form of it is, moreover, widespread among scientists themselves. It is not surprising, therefore, that intellectuals have tended to be alienated from a traditional religious outlook.

This tendency has been reinforced by social factors. The Industrial Revolution, which succeeded in any event upon a period of widespread indifference to religion in the eighteenth century, presented a double challenge to religion. On the one hand, the social disruption which it caused diminished traditional Christian allegiances: on the other hand, its miseries challenged the Churches in a new way. Though Christian social action was not wanting, it was inadequate, and by consequence Socialist and Marxist remedies provided a more hopeful and stimulating prospect of social betterment. Though these were not necessarily in conflict with religion (indeed, they were often inspired by the very motives which Christians ought to have held dear), in practice there was a split between the new prophets and the old priests. Thus Christianity sometimes seemed reactionary: it often seemed ineffective: it often appeared irrelevant. With the widening spread of higher education, so that the children of those already alienated from religion have strongly penetrated the literary and scientific worlds, it is understandable that the contemporary intellectual in Britain is typically indifferent to the Christian faith.

Nevertheless, such indifference is, of course, by no means universal. If many scientists are non-religious, others are not; if many teachers and professional people are alienated from Christianity, many others are not; if many writers and artists can see no force and plausibility in belief in God, others can. And we must not forget that a not inconsiderable number of university graduates have in this century been attracted by the doctrines of Marxism, which is itself in opposition to philosophical empiricism as understood by, say, Bertrand Russell. Marxism has its own metaphysics which in an important sense goes beyond science. It too can be thought of as a sort of religious system. Thus in one way or another a substantial proportion of intellectuals reject scientism. This leads us to examine seriously whether scientism is justified—whether it is indeed the rational option for "modern men". In the ensuing discussion, I shall, however, concentrate on the relation between scientism and Christian belief, though there are wider issues which could be discussed. I shall not, for instance, discuss it in relation to Marxism or to linguistic philosophy.

But before embarking on this discussion, it is as well to make some distinctions. The position which has here been called "scientism" is essentially a philosophical one. It is not the view that religion is wrong in this or that particular: it is the view that religion could not in principle be right, because it importantly has to do with God and God lies beyond the reach of scientific enquiry. Religion thus is in principle infertile—or, as has sometimes been said, it is meaningless.

This general philosophical view has to be distinguished from a more pragmatic one: namely, the view that religion could in principle be right but in fact is wrong, because it clashes with known scientific results. Thus if we took a literalist view of the Bible, it could be held that this was in conflict with modern biology and astronomy. The view amounts to saying: science has shown in various detailed ways that religion (the Christian religion as interpreted in such-and-such a way) is false. We may dub this view "pragmatic scientism" in contradistinction to "philosophical scientism".

This view in turn must be distinguished from a widespread sentiment, namely that if we want to get things done we should turn, not to religion, but to science. The fruits of technology are plain; those of religion are not. Science, in

the guise of technology, is the modern man's road to betterment. In comparison with it, religious aims shrink into in-
significance. We may dub this view "technological scientism".

Though the last two positions have a wide impact on
people's thinking, they represent a less fundamental intellectual challenge to religion than does philosophical scientism. It is thus convenient to discuss them more briefly first,
so that the decks can be cleared for the main combat.

First, technological scientism involves an essential misunderstanding of the Christian position. It is true that sometimes Christianity has appeared to offer magical rewards in
another world in place of the bread and wine lacking in
this. Sometimes, in the wrong way, Christianity has been
other-worldly, and therefore has encouraged the notion that
there is somehow a competition between the next world and
social betterment in this. Nevertheless, Christian theism
centres on two important ideas: first, that this world, being
created by God, is essentially good and valuable in its own
right; second, that God became incarnate in flesh and
blood, living and working in this world. Both ideas point to
the Christian's concern with human welfare. They both link
up with the parable of the good Samaritan. The Christian,
then, can be, and indeed ought to be, a co-worker with the
Creator in the continuing work of creation. Thus it is illusory to think of Christianity as being concerned with another world to the exclusion of the good things of this
world.

All this bears on the question of technology. For technology is practical: it is concerned with realising certain
ends or values. We build a bridge so that it is easier to cross
a river. We use reinforced concrete so that we can build
more strongly and higher. We use chemicals to fatten our
crops. If we did not want or need to travel, to have shelter,
to eat, these technological activities would become meaningless.

Now among our aims are those which we prize for their

own sakes; those which are themselves means to further ends; and those which are both (like kippers—good for keeping you active for the day's work, and enjoyable in themselves). Useful things are those which conduce to further ends, and we prize them because we prize those ends. This means that technology involves or presupposes a system of values, of ends which are regarded as good in themselves. These themselves need not be in turn useful (ultimately, indeed, the best things in life are useless, like cricket, music and worship). Thus in order to have a rational technology we must ask ourselves what system of ends it is that we are trying to realise. What are the values which technology subserves? Technology necessarily points beyond itself.

It is clearly nonsense to suppose, then, that technology itself incorporates a system of values which is in conflict with those of religion. It is nonsense to suppose that diesel-engines are unchristian, while organs are Christian. Our instruments are neither the one thing nor the other. It can only be the ends to which we put them that could be in conflict with Christianity.

Putting the matter more positively: the Christian, who is told to love his neighbour, can and should make use of the best technological means available. The cure of the sick, for instance, has been immeasurably improved by advances in the manufacture and discrimination of drugs and by new techniques of surgery. There is no such thing as a Christian or a Marxist technology: though there can be such a thing as technology used in the furtherance of Christian or Marxist values. Thus the first lesson to learn about technological scientism is that it represents a conflict which does not exist.

Further, it is not even the case that in regard to the system of values which we aim to realise through the application of technology there is necessarily much difference between a Christian and a non-Christian view. For many of the values we aim to realise are negative (the eradication of disease, the prevention of starvation, the reduction of accidents), and men of goodwill are pretty much agreed on what count as evils which have to be minimised or destroyed. Furthermore, the Christian, as much as the humanist, is concerned with the promotion of recognisable joys and creations, like picnics, Shakespeare, architecture and toys. Thus, to say the least, there will be an enormous overlap between the Christian and other systems of values.

Technology, then, is not in competition with faith—as though some men use diesels and others use prayers. (Though it is true that prayer has often been treated magically, as a form of pre-scientific technology, as when people imagine that by praying for rain rain will be more likely to come.) Technology is not a competitor of religion. It is only that the Christian will see his system of values as cast into a certain framework: the framework of relationship to God. The sensible question, then, to ask, in relation to technology, is this. What kind of a society—what sort of human values—are we trying to realise? This is a necessary question, since technology may come to be an end in itself, as though the gadget is more worth while than its function.

Pragmatic scientism is perhaps a more serious challenge than its technological brother. But it is a challenge for accidental reasons. Its power arises out of the history of the comparatively recent past: a period in which obscurantist interpretations of Christianity have in fact come into conflict with modern knowledge. The famous debate, in the last century, between T. H. Huxley and Bishop Wilberforce, on the origin of species, is a classical example of this. Some Churchmen, such as Wilberforce, thought it necessary to reject Darwinianism in the name of religion. The conflict between Galileo and the Church, though it did not turn solely on scientific issues, is another instance of the collision between religious conservatism and scientific discovery. Such instances have become deeply embedded in the folk-memory of modern man. He can be easily convinced thereby that religion has been "disproved" by science.

But such a conclusion is, of course, unwarranted for a

number of reasons. First, it depends on bad abstractions—
the abstraction of a monolithic religion and the abstraction
of a monolithic science. There were, for instance, biologists
who rejected Darwin and Christian thinkers who accepted
him. The collision essentially was between some scientists
and some Christians. Indeed, the whole talk of a "conflict
between science and religion" is crude and unhistorical.
Second, the conclusion is unwarranted because only a pretty
literalist account of Christianity can be disproved in this
way. If we were right in arguing in the previous Chapter in
favour of the new historical perspective on the Bible, and
in favour of the recognition of poetical and mythological
strands in the material, there is no need (quite the contrary)
to be exposed to this kind of conflict with scientific theories.
Third, as we shall see, the fact that theistic religion centres
on belief in a God who is "beyond" the cosmos will make it
unlikely that faith can be disproved by theories which explicitly confine themselves to the cosmos or to parts thereof.

On the other hand, as we have emphasised, Christianity
has a central historical dimension. It is perfectly true that
scientific history could in principle wreck Christian belief if
the main facts to which Christianity is anchored were
shown to be false. For instance, if we dug up some new and
more reliable document than the Gospels, and found that it
described Jesus as having wantonly murdered someone; or
suppose that it could be shown that Jesus never lived, but
was a myth and a fabrication of the early Church; suppose
such things were to be discovered, Christianity would
surely, and rightly, have to die. Christianity cannot in this
respect be immune to the evidence.

Nevertheless, we can safely say that pragmatic scientism
is not altogether convincing. But it raises questions.

For instance, the critic of religion may say this. "You
Christians were once pretty content to accept a fairly crude
interpretation of *Genesis*; now that the modern perspective
has shifted, through the scientific revolution, you are shifting
your ground. If you can get away with pre-scientific think-

ing, you do it; if you can't you blithely abandon it. Your 'modern' Christianity is nothing less than retreat forced upon you by external circumstances."

There is truth in these remarks. But is theological change disreputable? Is it so fatal to admit past errors? Is it absurd to incorporate modern insights into an ancient faith? Are "external circumstances" themselves somehow unchristian?

If we candidly accept that revision and reinterpretation are part of the process of thinking about the fundamentals of the Christian faith, and do not attempt to pretend that such revision has always come spontaneously within the Christian community, there can be no harm in rejecting pragmatic scientism. Or rather, there can be no harm in accepting that some cruder versions of Christian belief have been disproved by modern knowledge, while not accepting that thereby Christianity itself has been ushered out. Nor is such an attitude so revolutionary as some would imagine it to be. The Church has over many centuries—since its inception—attempted to relate its message to the knowledge of the day, in order that this message may be itself understood more clearly. If also the Church has been in many respects conservative (though in other respects dynamic), this is partly because an undue distinction has been made between "sacred" and "profane" knowledge, as though secular insights do not arise from the fabric of God's creation, and as though a sacred revelation is a static set of propositions. Fortunately, the internal dynamic of the Church's life has thrown up enough critics of the static view to save the Church from becoming an intellectual and spiritual ghetto.

In brief, then, pragmatic scientism is more a view which reminds us of the obscurantisms of the past than one which represents an essential challenge to a humane Christian belief.

There is one issue which lies at the border between pragmatic and philosophical scientism: the idea of miracles. It is an obvious feature of Christian belief that Christ, and others, performed miracles. The Resurrection itself has been interpreted as having a miraculous character. Scientific historians of the New Testament have thereby found themselves in a dilemma. On the one hand, there is the testimony of the documents, and the fact that if Jesus were all that is claimed of him the Resurrection *could* happen; on the other hand, the scientific historian would certainly not credit a miracle as the explanation of some event during the Crusades or what have you. The dilemma is mainly a philosophical one, but also it has to do with the canons of scientific history.

The most sensible first remark to be made about miracles is that on the whole they do not happen. This is part cause of the historian's dilemma concerning the Bible. It would be clearly rational for him to assume that some alternative explanation is correct, for instance in relation to the crossing of the Red Sea. On the other hand, to rule out the possibility of the miraculous in advance is to take up a philosophical stance. If, for instance, Jesus was divine it would be wrong to rule out the Resurrection in advance. Whether we envisage the possibility of miracles will turn on wider issues.

Briefly, they are these. First, a miracle is not just a highly unusual event; it also has a revelatory aspect. If a piece of fluff, contrary to known laws of nature, were to rise up to the ceiling and turn purple, this would doubtless be extraordinary; but it would not be a miracle in the sense in which the Bible speaks of the miraculous. To be a miracle, then, an event must have divine significance. It follows that we cannot seriously envisage the possibility of miracles unless we already accept the possibility of God's existence and activity. Consequently, the question of miracles is partly the wider question of the truth or otherwise of philosophical scientism.

Second, the general possibility of events which are "exceptions" to the laws of nature cannot be ruled out by appeal to science. Science no doubt, among other things, formulates laws of nature (of the form "Whenever such-and-such occurs, such-and-such occurs"), but these laws of nature are not, so to say, destroyed by single exceptions. For example, we would not abandon the Law of Gravitation simply because, say, the Ascension contradicts it: we would only abandon it if we could show that there was a class of experimentally repeatable events which failed to conform to the Law. In short, a law of nature is destroyed by a small-scale law, not by a single contrary instance. Thus belief in miracles is certainly compatible with a scientific attitude. Thus the general possibility of miracles is a question which has to be decided on grounds other than purely scientific ones.

But third, it should be noted that a scientific attitude does have a bearing on religious belief in so far as the latter may incorporate pre-scientific attitudes. For instance, the belief that certain forms of mental disease are caused by the operation of demons was widespread in New Testament times. Now, we would not think in these terms. At first sight belief in demons seems on a par with belief in the miraculous: but this is not really so. For the demon theory was the sketching of a pre-scientific law of nature, which, as it happens, we now reject. It was not a belief that a certain event was contrary to the expected course of nature. Thus we should distinguish between belief in miracles (which may or may not be justified on philosophical grounds) and pre-scientific beliefs (which tend to get replaced with the progress of science).

It will be apparent from the above arguments that the historian's dilemma on the miraculous cannot properly be resolved except through an examination of the plausibility of philosophical scientism. But we may note that since belief in the miraculous will in part depend on belief in God, rather than vice versa, it is useless to attempt (as used to be fashionable) to argue from miracles to the divinity of Christ and the truth of revelation. The argument would, if anything, have to be the other way round. This remark will, of course, tell us something about the way in which the Bible should be treated and taught.

Philosophical scientism can come in different varieties— tough and soft, crude and sophisticated. Perhaps its toughest and most sophisticated version is that found in A. J. Ayer's famous *Language, Truth and Logic*, published before the last war. Ayer was heavily influenced by the teachings of the so-called Vienna Circle, a group of philosophers interested in scientific method who had formulated an intellectual programme which would rid the philosophy of science from unwanted metaphysics. Indeed, the movement known as "Logical Positivism", which found its clearest expression in Ayer's book, conducted an all-out onslaught on metaphysics, and thus on a great deal of traditional philosophy. The weapon used in this onslaught was the Verification Principle, namely the doctrine that the meaning of a sentence lies in its method of verification (i.e. through observation or sense-perception). Those sentences (like "God created the world") which could not be verified in this way were thus considered to be meaningless. What is meaningless does not, of course, even get to the stage of being false. Nor was this criterion of meaning wholly implausible. For instance, suppose I say "There is a snark in the diningroom", and you go and look and discover no strange beast there. "There's no snark," you say. "There is," I reply: "you don't think I meant a *visible* snark, do you?" You go off to listen. "I can't hear anything," you say. "But I don't mean an audible snark," I say . . . and so on. By now, having evacuated from my claim anything which could be verified by observation, I have thereby eroded it of any real meaning.

The Verification Principle, then, had as one of its effects the claim that religious discourse is meaningless (save where, for instance, it is about Jesus as a human being). This represented a new agnosticism—not the Victorian agnosticism of saying that one did not have enough evidence to know whether it was true or false to say that God exists, but a logical agnosticism which claimed that it was neither true nor false to say that God exists, because it is meaningless.

The Verification Principle, however, ran into a number of technical difficulties. For one thing, it was too strong: for one cannot conclusively verify that the Law of Gravitation is true. To do so, it would be necessary to examine all instances of gravitation. This is impossible; and similarly with other laws of nature. Again, it was difficult to know what to make of inner events, such as my mental picture of Loch Lomond, since others cannot observe my mental picture, and my own awareness of it is not a matter of observation or sense-perception. Again, the Principle did not seem to accord too closely with the way we ordinarily use "meaning". In the ordinary sense, it certainly seems to have some meaning to assert that God was in Christ, etc. This difficulty could be evaded by saying that the Principle represents a recommendation on how to use the term "meaning": it represents a philosophical policy, rather than an analysis of how language ordinarily works. But then it could be asked: Why this policy rather than some other?

For these reasons, the Principle had to be modified, and there are few people, if any, who would now hold it in its old form. Nevertheless, the discussions it generated have formed an important element in modern philosophical discussions of religion. They have raised the fundamental question of whether our claims about the world, to be worth taking seriously, have to be in principle capable of being verified or falsified by the canons of scientific method.

Everyone, however, is not agreed as to what science is really like. Nevertheless, some general remarks about scientific enquiry will help to clarify the issues.

First, science is in an important way experimental. This is not to say that all science is experimental: clearly it is not. For instance, a history of the earth's geological structure is not: you cannot get the earth into a laboratory. Nevertheless, even the non-experimental aspects of science are heavily dependent on experiment. This is because the laws which we can test in the laboratory also operate outside it. For example, an account of the operation of the solar system is heavily dependent on gravitational theory, which itself has experimental justification.

Second, and partly because of this first aspect of scientific method, science is importantly *theoretical*. In general, fruitful experimentation occurs when an hypothesis is being tested. Such hypotheses can, up to a point, be confirmed (though not conclusively, for the reason cited earlier, on p. 47); and they can conclusively be falsified. For example, suppose my hypothesis is that litmus paper always turns purple when exposed to mustard-gas, and I find that repeatedly it does not; then, I have to drop or to modify my hypothesis. Modifying an hypothesis is in effect substituting a new one and dropping the old one. So negative evidence can make me abandon a theory.

Third, because of the necessity of hypotheses in science, there is an important way in which science goes beyond the evidence available: or rather, there are two ways in which it does so. Firstly, an hypothesis of the form "Whenever A occurs, B occurs" covers, or is intended to cover, all time and space: it covers an indefinite number of instances. I can never examine all these: the best I can do is to sample them. Thus a scientific hypothesis, generally speaking, goes beyond the evidence. Secondly, the way in which theories and hypotheses are born is not normally, if ever, by simple inspection of the data. Sometimes patterns of regularity will suggest an hypothesis: but very often the patterns are not seen till one begins testing a theory. Some of the most striking discoveries of science have occurred through a revolution in concepts, rather than through the accumulation of data. Consider Newton and Einstein, for example. We may refer to this aspect of science as its creativity—it is the active imagination of men that has so often wrested secrets from nature. It is not as though the monotony of natural events has forced the formulation of scientific laws upon men.

Fourthly, and in line with some of these other features, science is observational. This is implied by its experimentality, but the matter goes further. However important theories may be, they have to fit the facts. These facts are largely supplied by observation. Thus astronomy is not just the evolution of theories about the cosmos: it is importantly involved in observing the complexities of the cosmos. But it may be noted that observation is not a simple matter of looking: the more refined it is, the more heavily dependent it is upon instruments, like telescopes, microscopes and so on. We speak, for instance, of radio-astronomical observations, though what the radio-telescope is sensitive to is radio-waves, which cannot be seen. The pointer-reading on the dial, the pattern on the radar—these very often become more important than direct or magnified vision. Nevertheless, of course, in the end it is by our eyes and ears and other sense-organs that we come to check on the data supplied by the instruments. But it is worth noting that scientific "seeing" is very often a highly sophisticated sort of seeing. It is not like sitting in a garden idly contemplating a rose-bush.

To sum up: we have discriminated four important features of scientific method: its experimentality, its theoreticality, its creativity and its observationality. Given these features, philosophical scientism will have to involve the claim that religious propositions are empty or insignificant because religion is not experimental, or it is not theoretical, or it is not theoretically creative, or it is not observational.

Now no defender of religion, I suspect, would simply want to treat it as a branch of science. It is because religion is different from science that it has a point. And if it is a branch of science, it is a pretty rum one. Thus it is hardly reasonable to react to philosophical scientism by assimilating religion so closely to science that it loses its *raison d'être*. But it may not be so unreasonable to try to show that in certain respects there is an analogy with science. This may help to dispel the idea that while science deals with "hard facts", religion points to vapid illusions. It may help to dispel the idea that an acceptance of scientific method need not exclude belief in facts which lie, as it were, beyond science. (Though this beyondness is not a beyondness of superiority, nor does it enshrine the idea that if the scientists tried a little harder they would reach God: as though God were like an electron or a star.)

First, we may note that the theoretical and creative aspects of scientific method involve reaching beyond the experimental and observational evidence. This is why it is a more fruitful approximation to say that scientific claims are falsifiable in principle, rather than that they are verifiable. The Verification Principle of meaning has to be replaced by a Falsification Principle of method (as Karl Popper has argued). The scientific theory is one which is in principle sensitive to observational and/or experimental disproof.

But falsifiability is also a characteristic of Christian theism. We have already noted that new historical evidence could destroy the Christian gospel, if it demonstrated the unreality or wickedness of Jesus. But it may be objected that the doctrine of creation is not in the same boat. How could one ever disprove it? What observational evidence could ever knock it out?

The reply to this is two-fold. First, religious doctrines are in an important way organic. The Christian doctrine of creation comes to us as part of a certain fabric of belief in which different propositions are woven together and have a mutual interplay of meaning. The opening verses of St John's Gospel, for instance, try to see creation in the light of Christ, and Christ in the light of creation. In this respect, there is a certain analogy (but not a complete likeness) to scientific theories. For instance, in order to understand what a gene is, one has to understand a whole nexus of genetical theory. Likewise with electrons and radiation. These concepts are not simple labels for objects: they embody a whole lot of theory. Somewhat likewise, religious concepts like Christ the King, Creator and sacrament, need to be understood in terms of a whole set of doctrinal and historical affirmations. Thus, because of the interplay between the different parts of a doctrinal scheme, the whole scheme becomes an organic whole. The disproof of one important element in the scheme will have wide repercussions on the whole. Thus the Christian doctrine of creation borrows a degree of falsifiability from the doctrine of Christ.

Second, more generally, it is perhaps not necessary to confine our facts to those which can be observed, or connected theoretically to what can be observed. It remains merely a dogma to claim that all facts are facts about moons and flowers and humans and other denizens of the cosmos. There need be no general embargo upon belief in a transcendent reality, provided such belief is not merely based on uncontrolled speculation.

In two ways it is not. First, the existence of the cosmos itself may be held to require some sort of explanation, even though such an explanation will be necessarily non-scientific. We shall revert to this topic shortly. Second, belief in a transcendent reality is everywhere in religion connected with the idea that in one way or another this transcendent reality makes itself manifest, or is made manifest, to men. Belief in a transcendent reality is organically connected in Christianity, for instance, to the revelatory events in which God unveils himself. A merely "theoretical" or speculative belief in a transcendent reality would be vapid: but it does not happen to be the belief characteristicallly found in religion.

Consequently, there is a certain analogy between belief in the transcendent and scientific method. The religious believer goes beyond the evidence, and yet sees his "theory" in relation to concrete exents and experiences. In having faith in a transcendent realm he is exercising, one might say, a version of the creative imagination which plays such a central role in scientific discovery.

Yet of course in a number of respects religious belief

must remain different from science. It is different because revelatory events are not simply observations, nor is the exercise of the religious life a matter of scientific experimentation. Religious belief is different too because it uses categories such as holiness and worship which can play no part in science. The reasons for these differences are various. Partly, it is because religious theism by definition has to do with a holy and mysterious Being: the sense of divine mystery gives, as it were, a characteristic flavour to the religious man's attitudes. Partly, the difference arises because the object of theistic belief is a personal Being. Revelation is a form of communication between persons; it is a form of growing together between persons; it is a form of amity and love. But the interplay between persons, even in this world, is not just a matter of cool observation. My friend may have a wart on his nose: this is visible. But our understanding one another arises in part at least from the active mutual impingement of the one person on the other. Seeing the meaning of my friend's smile is more than a matter of seeing the way his lips curl upwards.

So far, enough perhaps has been said to indicate that philosophical scientism need not be accepted. It need not be accepted because the criteria we use for discriminating something as scientific also apply by analogy to religion. It need not be accepted because the exclusion of transcendent fact rests on a mere decision.

Moreover, the very excitements and creativities of science may induce in us a frame of mind where the extra dimension of glory in the universe constituted by God will not seem remote and implausible. The creativity of science gives it an open and adventurous character. Willingness to look beyond the stars and beneath the leaf into the hidden beauty of a transcendent world is only to transmute this adventurousness into a new key.

This is not to deny that all sorts of serious objections to Christianity can be brought; it is not to deny the disillusionment which many feel in contemplating Christian teachings and institutions. It is not to deny the dreary irrelevance which many find in religious faith. All that is here being affirmed is that the successes of science in no way afford a strong ground for refusing to see another dimension to existence—the transcendent dimension. If, then, someone decides that this extra dimension is but a vapid illusion, a creation, perhaps, of overwrought human phantasy; if such a decision is taken, it is itself a kind of act of faith. It is an act of faith in humanism or atheism. But this act of faith cannot be justified *a priori*: it must be a conscious act. It should not shelter behind an unthinking scientism, just as religious belief cannot shelter behind an unreflectively pre-scientific superstition.

Nevertheless, it is one thing to say that it is unadventurous and unreasonable to rule out in advance the possibility of a transcendent realm; it is quite another to say that there are good grounds for belief in the transcendent. So far we have merely been affirming the former thesis. We have been concerned with the possibility of a divine world, not with its actuality. What is to be said on the latter issue? What positive grounds are there for belief in a Creator?

The answer to this question will depend upon the decision we make as between revelationism and liberalism, as described in the previous chapter. If we adopt a revelationist position, then there are no grounds external to revelation itself for belief in God. If, on the other hand, we adopt the liberalist position, then we would expect to be able to cite reasons outside revelation for such a belief. Since the former option forecloses discussion, and since the latter does not, it is here best to explore the latter option. For the more possibility there is of discussion, the more scope there is for dialogue. The greater the possibility of reasoning, the greater the chance of an interplay between the "secular" world and the Church. The liberalist position, moreover, will in a sense be more congenial to the sceptical atheist, for it will propose some questions to him, rather than leaving him out in the cold. We shall, then, for the purposes of this argument adopt the liberalist position, and we shall attempt to see if there is any real possibility of a viable natural theology, starting from the world and pointing towards God.

In the past, a number of celebrated arguments have been used to try to prove the existence of God. A classical set is the so-called "Five Ways" (five arguments) of St Thomas Aquinas, who, of course, is the "official" philosopher of the Roman Catholic Church. Various of the traditional arguments have come under heavy critical fire from philosophers, including David Hume and Immanuel Kant. Some of the criticisms have been of a technical nature, and are none the worse for that, since the arguments themselves have often been rather technically presented. It would perhaps be gratuitous here to go through the various moves that have been made. Suffice it to say that the supposed proofs of God's existence are highly dubitable and that, on the other hand, they do express problems about the existence and nature of the cosmos which can rightly continue to engage our attention.

The two most important types of theistic "proof" are the so-called Cosmological and Teleological Arguments. The former argues that there must be a First Cause to explain the existence of the cosmos. The second argues that the signs of design in the cosmos show that there must be a Supreme Designer or Governor of the cosmos. A brief consideration of these claims will illuminate the question of how far a natural theology is genuinely possible.

The sentiment which the Cosmological Argument expresses is a powerful one. It is the feeling of astonishment which we may have in contemplating the possibility that the cosmos might not have existed at all. How far is this sentiment intellectually justified? It may seem to us amazing that there is something and not nothing; and we may thus obscurely suppose that an explanation of this is needful. But how far are we the victims of mere feeling here? Is there really a problem?

Perhaps we are just under the spell of an ancient way of thinking—that the world must have been made by someone. We may be just under the spell of the magical anthropomorphism of the primitive, which seeks to explain natural phenomena in terms of the activity of personal beings, thereby finding a homeliness and intelligibility in an otherwise inexplicable and hostile array of natural events.

Nevertheless, there are some intellectual reasons for holding that the existence of the cosmos represents a problem. For it seems just to say that the cosmos might not have existed at all. There is no contradiction involved in such an affirmation. Even supposing the cosmos is infinite both in time and space; even supposing that it always existed: even then, it seems possible that it might not have existed. Now when we come across a state of affairs which might not have obtained—for instance, that there are many trees in Norway—it makes sense to ask why it does obtain. It makes sense to ask why there are many trees in Norway, when there could have been one. Such questions may sometime be banal, but they remain meaningful for all that. Similarly, if the cosmos might not have existed, it is meaningful to ask why it does.

The hypothesis that the cosmos exists because of the creative activity of a personal God is perhaps not the only possible explanation. But it is one. Maybe it involves a leap beyond the evidence, but that, as we have seen, is not by itself a defect, for it is part of the typical nature of theories and explanations. The existence of a personal Creator, moreover, fulfils an important requirement of any explanation for the existence of the cosmos. For it would be no good explaining the existence of the cosmos in terms of a material object or force, like an immense magnetic field. For such a material object or force would itself, by definition, be part of the cosmos we are trying to explain. Thus in order to give an explanation of the cosmos we need to postulate some non-material being or force. The idea of a personal Creator fulfils this condition, and at the same time provides an analogy whereby we can begin to understand it. For in our own experience we are used to explaining certain events in terms of the agency of persons (as when we explain an explosion as being the result of an attempt to blow up the President). Such explanations differ from physical explanations (as when we explain the explosion as being due to the properties of gelignite under certain initial conditions). Thus the idea of a personal Creator simultaneously is recognisable as a kind of explanation and differs from physical explanations.

Thus the contingency of the cosmos—the fact that it might not have existed—creates a problem, one solution of which is the postulation of a personal Creator. Yet this in turn creates a problem. If the cosmos might not have existed, so equally the Creator might not have existed. Do we not then have to suppose that there is a Supercreator, who creates the Creator—and so on indefinitely? Are we then any better off? An intuition of this problem is already contained in the child's question as to who made God. And if we arbitrarily assert that there is at least one Being, namely God, whose existence does not require explanation, why should we not start earlier (like Spinoza) and assert that there is at least one Being whose existence does not require explanation, namely the universe? Can we not postulate that the cosmos is self-explanatory, and thereby forget all about a transcendent Creator?

Such an objection is powerful, but not altogether decisive. It is not decisive, because the crucial issue, in regard to explanations, is whether an explanation increases our understanding. We have to ask whether it brings any kind of advance in intelligibility. Now the simple affirmation that the cosmos' existence requires no explanation—that the cosmos is self-explanatory—does not help in regard to the problem with which the Cosmological Argument essentially starts. It does not serve to illuminate the question of why the cosmos exists, when it might not have existed. At best, it can be supported by an appeal to philosophical scientism: to appeal to the doctrine that because an explanation of the cosmos in terms of a transcendent Being is necessarily a non-scientific one it is therefore vapid and nugatory. But this is to beg the question, and the former discussion of philosophical scientism can recur profitably at this point.

On the other hand, the notion that the cosmos depends and has always depended on the creative activity of the Creator does bring some advance in intelligibility, even though this advance may seem to be limited. Consequently, it follows from the nature of explanations that as an explanation the doctrine of a Creator has the edge over the affirmation that the cosmos is self-explanatory. It does not stop the "why?" off at its source. It does not stultify our intellectual unease. It holds a certain shadowy promise. To this extent, it is a rational option. But still there remains the sinister string of Supercreators. Do we want to be landed with such metaphysical and theological complications? The answer to this is fairly simple. For what role do the Supercreators play in advancing our understanding? So far very little. The step from cosmos to Creator is momentous: the step from Creator to Supercreator is at best murky. Of course, if there are theological or other reasons for postulating a God above God, and some thinkers have argued in this way, the Supercreator may come into his own. But otherwise the Supercreator remains a rather barren speculation, a shadowy testimony to the force of the child's question.

Now no one would be inclined to suppose that the above defence of the essential point of the Cosmological Argument is anything other than tentative. No one would mistake it for a "proof" of God's existence. Rather, it is an attempt to provide some rationale for natural theology. It is an attempt to show that we can begin from the world about us and move towards belief in God. It is an attempt to show that theism begins to solve the problem posed by the sense which we have, or may be brought to have, of the contingency of the world.

It is in any event somewhat odd to seek what is strictly a proof of God's existence. Does the Christian have to prove God's existence, when he already communes with God? And will the atheist or agnostic be simply persuaded by formal argument? What we may hope to prove is still only a First Cause or a Designer of the world: and yet for the theist the proof would have to go much further. The proof would have to be a proof of the God of Abraham, the God who was in Christ. We have to leap, as it were, beyond what our premisses strictly warrant. We have to go, as in science, beyond the immediate evidence. Such a leap is hazardous, and is not susceptible of strict demonstration. It is unrealistic to expect anything else. The quest for the knockdown proof in religion is absurd and, probably undesirable.

If God had wished to make himself unmistakably known: if he had desired that men should accept his existence and revelation unhesitatingly: if religion were something which could be forced upon our intellects in this way: then surely God would have arranged the stars to spell out the Creed. He would have written St John's Gospel on vegetable leaves, so that every kitchen-gardener in the world could testify to the unmistakable revelation of God. He would have overwhelmed men with a display of miraculous pyrotechnics. We may ask: why is all this not so? From the Christian point of view it is surely significant that God has moved in mysterious ways. It is surely significant that the kind of "revelation" which we have postulated would betray both the nature of God's mysteriousness and the free faith of men. God would collapse into a literal-minded Being, and with that collapse the deeper dimensions of faith, adoration and discipleship would themselves vanish. To ask for such "proof" is to ask for the wrong thing. It is to ask for a stone when it is bread that is at issue. It is to misunderstand the nature of religion, and the nature of God's self-revelation. For these reasons, it is not to be regretted that at the metaphysical level there are no knockdown arguments for God's existence.

Nevertheless, as we have seen, God's existence is a possibility suggested by the contingency of the cosmos. Hence, the reply to a crass scientism or an unreflective atheism which dismisses *a priori* the transcendent dimension of reality is to stimulate a proper and vital sense of the contingency of the world. This is why the conscious atheist may on occasion be nearer to faith than the unreflective or wooden-hearted Christian. For instance, Sartre, the French Existentialist, is vividly aware of the absurd: of the absurdity of man in an inexplicable, Godless world. Sartre is well aware of the meaningless contingency of things, and is at the same time, and partially thereby, aware of God. In being aware of God's absence from the universe he is in a way aware of his presence. Thus a reflective and sensitive atheism is to be preferred to a dull acceptance of cosmic prejudices, whether Christian or not. It is not altogether a paradox to answer the question "And how do we teach natural theology?" with the reply: "By teaching atheism".

The root, then, of the Cosmological Argument is the unease produced by the contemplation of the possibility that the cosmos might not have existed. This is a more radical unease than the old question "What started the world going?" It is a more radical unease than that induced by the thought that the world must have a beginning in time. The Cosmological Argument in this form is equally applicable whether or not the cosmos is infinite in time— whether or not it started a finite number of years ago. The doctrine of Creation, moreover, is not what a superficial reading of *Genesis* might imply. It is not just (if at all) the doctrine that God started things off in the beginning, with a big bang or whatever. It is on the contrary the doctrine that the world is continuously dependent for its existence upon God's activity. It is the doctrine that God is the continuous creator of the world. To hold the other view is to get into a position which has been long seen to be nugatory and untheistic: it is to adopt a Deistic view—as though God, having got the machine going, left it to its own devices, occasionally tinkering, however, when it gave off funny noises. Basically, it is the view that God is an absentee Creator. This is not the belief of the Bible. Nor is it intellectually satisfactory to postulate a Creator for such a limited task. Nor is it a view which is religiously very significant, for it does not express the full force of God's presence operatively throughout his world. It does not stimulate the imagination to see the continual glory of the creative power shining through the events which surround us. For all these reasons, it must be emphasised that the Cosmological Argument points to a continuous dependence of the cosmos on God, and that the idea of such a Creator is compatible both with the theory of a finite universe and with the theory of an infinite one. It is neither hostile to Hoyle nor to Gamow. It is neutral as between scientific cosmologies. (This does not prevent some folk from thinking, wrongly, that the Steady State Theory of the universe, according to which the cosmos is infinite in time, "disproves" *Genesis*: again we note the horrid tendency of atheists and Christians alike to treat that long-suffering book as though it should have been published by the Cambridge University Press as a popular paperback on science.)

In brief, the Cosmological Argument—beginning with the question "Why does the cosmos exist?"—provides a stimulus towards accepting the idea of a Creator. It provides us with a non-revelational reason for taking the question of Creation seriously. It is no proof; but it is an unease.

The Teleological Argument, which begins from the evidence of design and order in the cosmos, has, if anything, come under stronger fire from philosophers than has the Cosmological. One reason is that there is apparently quite a lot of disorder in the world. Another is that the Argument has sometimes been naïvely applied. For instance, it has been argued that the cunning way the eye has been put together, and the marvellous arrangement of the tiger's muscles—that these phenomena show that a Designer must somehow have done the job. Darwinianism and other developments have cast the strongest doubt on such appeals to "common sense". Moreover, the idea of purpose, which was prominent in the biological thinking of Aristotle and many of his successors, has been quietly removed from scientific speculation. It seems more profitable to look at biology in terms of mechanisms than of purposes. For these and other reasons it is no longer fashionable to see particular purposes at work in the world.

Nevertheless, the Teleological Argument can draw our attention to a feature of the cosmos: namely, that it is rather orderly. The regularities of natural events may contrast with a certain randomness to be discovered there too; but the regularities provide the framework for the randomnesses. The cosmos could indeed have been a good deal more disorderly. For instance, it might have consisted in atoms wandering about along random paths. It might have been, as it were, a grey fog. As it is, it is organised to such a degree that sophisticated organisms, such as ourselves, are viable. It is orderly enough to make intelligence and consciousness possible. These facts by themselves do not go to prove anything. But if we already feel open to the conclusion that there is a Creator, we may feel entitled to argue that the degree of orderliness in the world points to the Creator's prizing of what we prize. The reasons for this perhaps surprising claim are as follows.

We sometimes think that values are, so to say, built into the nature of reality. We sometimes hear folk say that this is a "moral" universe. It sometimes looks as though our duties and rights derive from the inner nature of the world. Such a notion of "objective" values is, however, doubtful (and later this issue will be discussed in a little more detail). What seems, however, obvious—whatever view we take of the nature of moral and other values—is that they are nothing without conscious beings. Beauty is in this respect relative to the beholder. Do we bury the beauties of the

Impressionists in caves? Do we put orchestras in sound-proof boxes? Has duty any meaning if there is no one to recognise what his duty is? Can there be love in the absence of both lover and beloved? The wonders of the silent starry night would no doubt exist, in a certain sense, without conscious beings to behold them. But values, to be realised, must be realised through conscious beings. That the world is a place which is regular enough to give birth to and to support such conscious beings is suggestive that the Creator of such a cosmos is not without regard for values. This is why the regularity of the cosmos suggests that God prizes what we prize (though no doubt not in detail: could he approve of such a boring pastime as bingo? Who knows?).

But let us not exaggerate the force of these considerations. The idea that the orderliness of the world is by itself a good argument for a Creator is extremely doubtful. But the orderliness of the cosmos may reinforce in some slight degree the hypothesis that the First Cause is of a personal nature.

Such then are certain ways in which one can lead in from the contemplation of the natural world towards a belief which finds its chief expression in revelation. Such are the ways in which a moderate natural theology can help to show that the teachings of theism throw light on problems raised by the existence and nature of the cosmos. Once again it needs stressing that we are far here from the area of proof.

Both in relation to the Cosmological Argument and in relation to the Teleological the essential task seems to be to arouse a genuine sense of wonderment. We are normally so wrapped up in our own and others' affairs that we take the framework against which we live for granted. We accept the cosmos dumbly and dully; we accept the existence of persons likewise. We do not pause to marvel at the odd strangeness of our predicament. We scarcely pause to realise that we are conscious beings moving in a world of unconscious leaves and stones. We do not remember to look at ourselves in wonderment. At a superficial level, why should we wonder? We are most of us no great marvels; and we expect people to think and feel. But here familiarity perhaps has bred contempt. Once we move away from our ordinary pursuits and concerns; once we are, as the saying is, "taken out of ourselves"; once we come critically before death and before the creation of life; once we contemplate ourselves from afar; once these things happen, we may perhaps feel the unease and the puzzlement that are the beginnings, not only of philosophy, but of sensitive religion and atheism as well. But it is not easy to create this wonderment; for even to say "What a wonderful piece of work is man!" can be a hollow and dull ejaculation. We can strive to cause wonderment in an unwondering way. We can always be victims of the cliché, just because the most exciting thing can be made boring in repetition and dulled by unimaginativeness.

The use of such natural theology as has been outlined above helps to reinforce the reasons for rejecting scientism. Even if by themselves the arguments are not strong in establishing a Creator, they provide hints. They are suggestive. They help to make it more plausible to look to the transcendent dimension. They militate against the embargo on the transcendent placed by a restrictive scientism. Thereby they may go some way towards showing that an antireligious climate of opinion does not rest on a very solid theoretical foundation.

It might perhaps be thought, however, that the discussion of the relation between science and religion in this chapter has been somewhat philosophical and abstract, and that thus it is hard to relate it to the questions ordinarily asked in this area. This view is, I hope, mistaken. It will be obvious that the discussion has indeed touched on the very questions which people and children, often in a rather unsophisticated way, raise. But to make the relation rather more direct, I propose to consider how the clichés and questions which most naturally occur to people can be countered and answered, and how a number of ordinary reactions can be themselves used to liberate ourselves from a restricted view both of science and religion. I propose to do this in the form of a brief dialogue. This is in effect a series of aphorisms and counter-aphorisms.

AN APHORISTIC INTERLUDE

A. "The Bible says that the world was created in a few days, but science says . . ."

B. "You say 'The Bible says', but you should instead consider what the Bible means."

A. "But Christians have said that the world was created in a few days, but science says . . ."

B. "Criticise Christians, if you will; they are fair game and deserve it, but we are also interested in the truth."

A. "If it is the truth you want go to science."

B. "And nowhere else? Not to religion?"

A. "Well, religious people have said a lot of things. How do we know they are true? But science has established firm results. You can test what it says."

B. "I can? How can I?—I who have no degree in physics."

A. "Well, look at the Bomb. Look at the things science can do for us. They show that science is on the right track; but what can religion do for us?"

B. "The Church is not a diesel-factory. What kind of business do you think it is in?"

A. "Still, if you are interested in human welfare, you do not look to heaven, but to earth."

B. "Heaven is all around us; so what direction do you think the Christian is looking?"

A. "Even so, science gets results."

B. "We are all pleased. No doubt we shall get round to knowing how best to use those results."

A. "But if we are all pleased, we're not in conflict. Why then bother me with faith?"

B. "If you want the truth, you have to be bothered even by falsity."

A. "But religion is out of date: as I said, it does not get established results. It is all so much talk and speculation."

B. "It is talk about heaven and talk about God. Does that damn it?"

A. "You can see the planets; you can see what science is about. You can't see God."

B. "Who said you should expect to see God?"

A. "This unseen world—it is meaningless; if you can't check up on it, anyone can say what he likes."

B. "So our only knowledge is of what can be seen?"

A. "That's how I feel. You can at least know what's what."

B. "Have you seen an atom?"

A. "No, but the experts believe in them."

B. "But they go beyond what they can see. Consider the Wilson Cloud Chamber."

A. "Maybe they go beyond what they can see, but they can test their theories by what they can see."

B. "God reveals himself in Christ; you can see Christ."

A. "But you can't trust the books. Look at the New Testament: turning water into wine—I ask you!"

B. "Well, the expert historian can sift the wheat from the chaff. Don't tell me you disapprove of the expert."

A. "They're biased sometimes. Anyway, what would Christianity be without Jesus rising from the dead? Who is going to believe that sort of thing?"

B. "Who was Jesus, by the way?"

A. "I know what the Church says. But if you don't believe in God, you can't accept that stuff."

B. "And if you could accept that stuff?"

A. "Then I'd listen to the Resurrection. But the water and wine and walking on the water . . ."

B. "But as it is, there is no God?"

A. "I don't know: I don't accept it, though. How should I know?"

B. "How did Newton know about gravitation?"

A. "Well, he didn't know, but he got the idea, and it turned out he was right."

B. "You have to get the idea of heaven all around us: you have to get the idea of the unseen world: you have to get these ideas if you want to know something of God."

A. "All right, so I get the ideas. How do I know they have anything in them?"

B. "You have to look to revelation, no doubt. But first you can look to the world."

A. "But I told you I believe in what can be seen. I accept the world."

B. "But the world as it is is not quite acceptable."

A. "You mean you don't like it? You Christians are always disapproving of things. Don't tell me you disapprove of the world!"

B. "On the contrary, I love it: it is full of heaven. But it is a puzzlement. What brought it into being? Why does it exist?"

A. "It just exists."

B. "I thought you loved science. What if Fleming, on finding his penicillin, had just said: 'Ah, some new substance. It exists.'?"

A. "Well, I don't know why the world exists."

B. "It might not have existed. Is that not food for thought?"

A. "All right, I am thinking."

B. "The Christian says it exists because of God's creative work."

A. "I know that, but it is only a theory. It's only a guess."

B. "A guess may be right."

A. "But what made God? Your theory is incomplete, if you ask me."

B. "God made and makes the world: that tells me something. That a God makes God tells me very little."

A. "If your theory is like that, why don't you rest content with saying that the world makes itself? That's a possible theory too."

B. "I don't deny it. But we know that the world exists; and it might not have; so we want to know why it does. It does not help much to say 'It exists because it exists'. Such a 'theory' is totally useless. At least mine advances matters a little."

A. "All right; your guess has something. But what is it to me if some unknown X or other created the world?"

B. "What indeed? But the God of Christianity is not an unknown X."

A. "Now you're talking the usual stuff about revelation."

B. "Do you expect me not to be? If God does not reveal himself, religion is pointless. Religion is about people. About us and about him. In relationship."

A. "I don't accept all that stuff in the Bible."

B. "I was not wanting to persuade you of that. Maybe it is not for me to do so. But you've changed."

A. "Changed?"

B. "You talk as though the heaven all about us is at least a possibility. Scientifically, you go beyond science, I suspect."

A. "Maybe I think it is possible: but I do not believe it. I stay with my atheism."

B. "But what sort of atheism? How does man fit into this?"

A. "Man? Yes, man is in a funny position. He thinks all this about God. He thinks about religion. But after all, he is left here in the world. A pretty empty world. It is lucky we have made it as human as it is."

B. "Now you speak like a real atheist: we are drawing closer together."

A. "If the thought pleases you, I shall not deny it."

CHAPTER FOUR

CHRISTIAN BELIEF AND THE NATURE OF PEOPLE

I<small>F</small> the doctrine of Creation has a considerable relevance to the physical sciences, the idea of salvation has a special relevance to our understanding of people. Since the Biblical revelation finds its climax, from the Christian point of view, in the deeds and death of Christ, whereby in some manner people are saved, it is necessary to be clear on what sort of a thing salvation is. The discussion of this will lead us far afield, since the idea of salvation presupposes a conception of the human predicament. Naturally, however, there are different interpretations of this predicament, and the present argument is merely designed to create the stimulus for individual decisions about this matter. It is designed to help towards clarification: it is in no way the enunciation of some definitive orthodoxy (in any case, I am no prelate!). The discussion is designed, then, to present possibilities, which will be indirectly relevant to the teaching of religion.

For many people, the idea of salvation is about the least relevant of Christian teachings. Since it stands at the heart of those teachings, this paradox requires some explanation. The reasons for it are probably these. First, without a vivid belief in God, it is impossible to feel the need for salvation, for salvation has to do with the relationship between people and God. Since many people do not have this awareness, they will fail to be enthused by the thought of salvation. On the other hand, the magnificent moral teachings contained in the Gospels can appeal to sceptics and agnostics, since they retain a force in their own right, despite the disappearance of belief in God.

Secondly, popular attitudes to salvation have been in part shaped by a certain sort of evangelism, which persistently asks "Are you saved?" This highly individualistic interpretation of salvation is not likely to inspire people who are well aware of the social dimension of human troubles. It smacks of minor changes of heart, when men cry out for a wider justice and a reshaping of society.

Thirdly, there is a common tendency to equate sin with immorality or unethical conduct. This suggests that the problem of salvation is the problem of how to be good. Since many people believe that one can be good equally well without religion, it is a natural inference to think that some technical, churchy sort of salvation is irrelevant or superfluous.

These reasons for indifference to the idea of salvation are in a backhanded way illuminating. For they provide us with three principles for controlling our approach to this doctrine. First, salvation should be seen clearly in terms of a new relationship to God. Second, it should be seen both in individual and social terms. Third, it should be seen as something distinct from the performance of good works.

All these principles can be illustrated from the concept of sin. It is, as has been hinted, unfortunate that sin has tended to become equated with immorality. It is unfortunate that as a further consequence it has become fragmented (so that one can speak of "sins", and even grade them in order of seriousness). These developments are unfortunate in that they tend to draw attention away from the essential roots of the idea, as found in the Biblical tradition and elsewhere. For the concept of sin is the converse of the conception of holiness. In the primary sense of the latter term, it is God who is supremely (and uniquely) holy. He is mysterious, powerful, sublime, glorious. It is by contrast with this vision of God's awe-inspiring holiness that men are treated as sinful. They are sinful because they are alienated from God: they fail to participate in his holiness and glory. They see, in the mirror of God's holiness, their own lack of glory. Thus a proper understanding of the idea of sin presupposes a conception of God's holiness. Sin is thus relative to God: it is not just failure to be good (for such failure can be seen without any explicit reference to the idea of God).

Secondly, it is part of the Biblical concept of sin that it is not just an individual phenomenon. Alienation from God occurs collectively, as well as individually. Sometimes the collective is Israel: sometimes more widely it is the human race. As we might say in modern terms: sin has a social dimension. The collective involvement in sin has been given a mythological expression through the story of the Fall of Adam—Adam the prototype of men, who thereby are implicated in the alienation from God.

Thirdly, the cure for sin is not simply moral and political reform. Though the Prophets thundered away at Israel for its ethical shortcomings, and tried to show that relationship to God must bring with it moral loyalty to God, the wiping away of sin, the restoration of men to wholeness and to intimacy with God, is to be effected by direct changes in the relationship between God and man. Thus at a relatively primitive level, sacrifice was thought to effect this. By expiation man is restored to a relationship in which God's wrath is averted. At a deeper level, according to the New Testament, it is through the work of Christ himself that man's whole position is transformed. God himself undertakes the sacrifice.

Yet when all this is said, there remains a problem of giving such notions a realistic interpretation in the contemporary world. We may see Christ's death as a sacrifice, but we no longer see this against a background of real blood sacrifices. For us the imagery of the "blood of the lamb" has largely lost its impact. For us, ideas of ritual uncleanness, which often entered into ancient thought about sin, are largely irrelevant. For us, because of changes in the meaning of the word, the term "sin" itself can give wrong impressions. Again, we may be sceptical about the mythology of Adam as the prototype of man. If we want to speak about mankind, we do not speak of an Adam. We speak of mankind. The disappearance or erosion of older categories therefore presents a real challenge in the interpretation, for our days, of these concepts.

It may be objected that if the description of the disease of which salvation represents the cure is outmoded, then there is no need to worry about being cured. If there is no disease, why look for treatment? But this objection overlooks the fact that the narrative of Adam and the whole nexus of related ideas are an attempt to express a certain moral and spiritual predicament which men have found themselves in. There is no special reason to suppose that social and human facts have changed so radically that the predicament has vanished. It is only that we may seek to understand it in language which makes more sense with the change in attitudes consequent upon the evolution of contemporary society and, indeed, with the experience and impact of Christianity over a period of nearly two thousand years.

The predicament can be put in the following way. For those who have an awareness of God as the holy Creator of the world there is a double tension. On the one hand the vision of the majestic glory and goodness of God leads to worship: and worship in turn expresses a recognition of God's supreme value. This recognition makes God our ideal: we seek to be like him. We seek to participate in his holiness. We seek to join in his creative work. On the other hand, the very nature of God—God's very holiness—seems to cut him off from us. This sentiment is vividly expressed in the account, for instance, of Isaiah's vision in the Temple. We seek holiness, then; but true holiness is out of our reach.

This is part of the predicament, and it seems a necessary one. Yet also the Christian revelation has suggested that sin, or estrangement from God, is not necessary—that it is the result of man's own choice. Adam was deliberately disobedient. It is common to think of man as typically a rebel against God. The story of Israel is replete with instances of the condemnation of a recalcitrant nation. And yet there are certainly difficulties in the way of counting the estrangement from God as simply a matter of recalcitrance.

For one thing, it is difficult to make sense of deliberate rebellion against a Being who is not known to the rebel. There is ample evidence that vast numbers of men, from very early times, have had no concept of a monotheistic God. Again, men have sometimes had a wrong picture of the one God. Is rebellion against that picture rebellion against God? Again, how can the disobedience of Adam implicate me?

It is at this point that we will probably begin to think that it is better to start with an analysis of the human condition than with an attempt at an historical account of men's estrangement. For only if we are clear about the analysis can we begin to make sense of the history. It needs repeating that the Biblical conceptions themselves were a poetical and mythological expression of what was felt as a contemporary predicament.

Two great qualities characterise men, qualities which we can refer to as vision and love. The remarkable achievements of mankind in art, in science, in literature, in agriculture, in industry—these achievements are a main consequence of vision. Those early folk who fashioned flinty tools, as well as those latter-day scientists who probe into the genes, displayed a vision beyond their immediate impressions. New ways of looking at the world have brought inventions and discoveries: they have brought intellectual and artistic revolutions: they have enriched both materially and spiritually the world of men: they have enlarged existence, and clothed life in new possibilities. In all this, men show their creativity. If there is one way in which man is made in the image of the Creator, it must be this.

Such vision is complemented by the human capacity for love. If vision clothes life in new possibilities, love prizes life itself. It brings men the warmth of intimacy, and it provides a spur for sacrifice. It gives a basis for the good society. It provides a framework for the exercise of vision, as vision provides a new milieu for love.

But love and vision are not just individual in their significance. They are nurtured and diffused by society. For instance, the vision of Einstein started from the achievements of earlier physicists, and has become diffused through institutions of learning and research. Likewise, love is promoted within the family and within the wider bonds of society, and it rebounds on them. The social dimension of vision and love is of profound importance, and an individualistic estimate of men's capacities is unrealistic.

On the other hand, we know well that vision and love are matched by other qualities: by blindness and hate. We know well that men are often prompted to fearful destructiveness, and are often blind to the possibilities of creation. The present century has shown us in stark fashion the black and stupid side of man. Both in society and as individuals we are often unfeeling, unimaginative, unmerciful, trivial, crass, gross, destructive, suspicious, prickly, guilty, angry. Our impulses and our institutions so often stand in the way of love and vision. Our ideals are blocked and buried. Hope is smothered in petty pride; vision is misted by greed; love is shot through with suspicion. We change the world, but not quite in accord with the good.

This again is not just a matter of individual blindness and hate. Very often our predicament is determined by the social and cultural situation. We are brought up to hate as well as to love: and our lack of vision is often determined by the ignorance of our society. We do not individually control the institutions which partially control us. The diseases of blindness and hate are as much organic social diseases as they are diseases of the individual. This is why the reform of mankind must always advance on two fronts: the individual must come to see the good, but the economic and social institutions themselves must be altered.

I expect most people would agree, in rough outline, with the above analysis (partly because it is a little vague). One does not need to be a Christian or a theist to see the glories and the ills of mankind. But the analysis will be useful in making sense of the old idea of sin.

In the first place, the vision and love which men can display reflect the central character of God, as Creator and as Love. The work of being co-operator with God in creation and love is already in part fulfilled through the exercise of these human capacities, whether or not men see themselves in that role. In this respect, estrangement consists in the forces of blindness and hate which block men's free advance to a wider and a deeper life. Thus the overcoming of this estrangement is through the work of liberation from blindness and hate.

From the Christian point of view, this liberation is through the work of Christ. But how is this? Classical theories of the Atonement have seen Christ's life, death and resurrection in a number of ways: as the cheating of the Devil of what he thought was his due; as the expiatory sacrifice which outweighs men's sins; as a supreme moral example; and so on. These theories (and none has been given the status of Church doctrine) need to be seen in the light of the actual human predicament. They are, indeed, inadequate. Jesus is a moral example, yes; but his saving work cannot just be this (for Socrates is a fine example too). A saving work must be effective, and how do I know that I shall be effectively inspired by Jesus' example? Again, if God wished to forgive sin, he could do so without a sacrifice. Again, the mythology of the Devil needs to be co-ordinated to the concrete situation in which people find themselves, and this is a hard task. But as we shall see, such classical theories testify to some important features of

Christ's work. Yet we still may ask: how does Jesus save us from the forces of blindness and hate? In what way was his life a liberation?

Partly, it was because that life demonstrated something. It showed something. It was not just an example of how humility and heroism can be blended, though it was also that. At a deeper level, it was a demonstration that God as Creator is also in a state of solidarity with man in his blindness and hate and suffering. Thus the vision and love of God is not something aloof; God does not leave men to their own struggling devices. He demonstrates through Jesus that while men may aspire to the heights, God descends to meet them in their entangled struggle. Thus the life of Jesus itself demonstrates men's creative role.

A demonstration can give hope: but hope does not overcome everything. A second feature of the Atonement, as hinted at in the theory of expiatory sacrifice, is this. The forces of blindness and hate induce despair and fear. For the Christian, who identifies vision and love with God's work, the despair at failure and the fear of alienation from God need no longer have power. In older terms, men's sin is outweighed by the infinite sacrifice of God on the Cross. And why? Because Jesus' work is the beginning of the creation of a new society, the "Kingdom". This new society is one in which the Christian can participate in the life of God. Through this participation, there is direct assurance of creative co-operation with God. The vision and the love move to the centre, while the despair and fear no longer have significance. Faith in the new society makes despair unreasonable; the bonds of love make fear of alienation from God illusory. The new society will go forward, and the old story of triumph over the Devil means that the forces of blindness and hate will ultimately be destroyed. The coming of Jesus has brought the victory, for it has brought the new society.

Is this new society the Church? Here we come down to earth with a bump! The story of the Atonement seems to have petered out into the sands of an uninspiring institution. What have the candles, the bickerings, the restrictions, the bad music, the conservatisms, the mumblings—what have these to do with the new society? Are we now to say: the grand solution to the problem of man's estrangement from vision and love is this—join the Church?

The grand solution cannot be simply this, for two reasons. First, the new society is not to be identified with the membership of the Church: some members of the Church are in it for conventional and other unsatisfactory reasons. Second, vision and love are to be found far beyond the bounds of membership of the Church.

Why then should the Christian regard the Church as important? Partly because the Church, for all its evils, has succeeded in transmitting the Gospel: it has been a vehicle of revelation. Its internal dynamic has prevented the Gospel from being totally obscured by human dreariness and ill-intent. Without the Church there would be no proclamation of Jesus (indeed, where there is this proclamation, there, in a sense, is the Church).

A second reason why Christians regard the Church as important is that in it there is possible an assured and intimate communion with God. The sacraments—however they may be interpreted—are an outward sign of this organic link between Christ and those who have faith. For these reasons, the Church may not be the new society: but it cannot be absent from the new society.

All this implies something more about Christ's work of salvation. It is not merely a demonstration of the divine solidarity with man's struggle as co-worker in Creation; it is not merely the creation of a new society in which despair and fear become peripheral; it is also the coming into existence of a new and more intimate relation between God and man. The distance and estrangement implied by the worship of God and the failures in human response are overcome in the act of God in taking on the weaknesses of the human condition. This is more than a negative act: a curing of man's condition by an expiatory sacrifice: it is rather the positive creation of a special relationship. Christ's work of salvation thus becomes a new creation: the heightening of divine-human love.

We may now place the above remarks in the context of the three principles elaborated earlier for a proper understanding of sin or estrangement. We can place them in the context of the theses that estrangement has a primary relation to God; that it is not merely an individual matter; and that salvation is not just a matter of good works.

First, we have tried to show that estrangement can be viewed at two levels as related to God. At one level, it is estrangement from vision and love—qualities which reflect the nature of the Creator. At another level, the overcoming of estrangement is by the creation of that new relationship with God in Christ which was brought into being through the Incarnation.

Second, the notion of estrangement has a collective and social aspect, again at two levels. On the one hand, lack of vision and love, and the forces of blindness and hate, are as much precipitated in individuals by their social milieu as conversely. On the other hand, the triumph which overcomes such estrangement comes through participation in the new society.

Third, salvation is not just a matter of good works, for a number of reasons which emerge from the above analysis. Both vision and love involve imagination, and such imagination fires men to act in accord with their vision and love. This inspiration is what needs to be nurtured, and from it works will surely flow. But works divorced from vision and love become wooden and dreary. Consider what it is like if a father says: "If it were not my duty to look after my children, I'd let them go." This indicates a defect in relationship. Of course, it is nice that he recognises his social duty; but we recognise the superiority of a relationship where the father says: "A duty to look after my children? I'd never thought of it in that way. Isn't it enough that I love the little monsters?" It is better, we think, when a person has his heart in his work or in his relationships. Not only will the work and the relationships thereby be better; but the man too, for his values and his life are thus far in harmony.

Again, salvation by works is not possible because of the nature of the relationship between God and man created by God's act in incarnation. This relationship, we have argued, involves a loving communion between God and men. Because the relationship is personal, there is an analogy with human relationships like friendship. One helps a friend because of the friendship. This friendship arises from the mutual magnetism of two personalities. Similarly, God's magnetism draws men to him. We cannot deliberately choose to have "faith" in God, for real faith is a response to God's person. The response may be nurtured and awakened by choices; but in essence it is not created by them. This is relevant too to the idea of revelation. God's self-manifestation, for example in Christ, is more than the unveiling of the truth. It is not just a matter (if it is this at all) of imparting information about himself. It is rather God's coming forward—his introducing himself. Thereby the possibility of faith is created.

A third main reason why salvation is not a matter of good works arises from the limited way in which "good works" tends to be interpreted. It was, for instance, the idea among some Pharisees (though not all)—notably it was the idea of St Paul before his conversion—that exact fulfilment of the Law would ensure salvation. Now this Law consisted both of ethical and ritual injunctions. Let us concentrate on the former, since ritual rules are not a prominent feature of our own society. Now it is quite clear that a system of moral rules (against stealing, murder, and so forth) is a necessary basis for social living. It is a necessary basis too for the existence of at least a limited justice, in which men are protected from the grosser damages which their neighbours may inflict upon them. All this is obvious.

But adherence to the rules is compatible with lack of vision and love; and it is compatible with blindness and hate. It is compatible with blindness, because we can adhere unthinkingly to a set of tabus without an insight into what gives them importance. We cannot see, for instance, that the principle of loving one's neighbour, which lies behind morality, demands that rules should be reviewed in the context of human welfare. Jesus himself, for instance, had such a revolutionary concept of moral rules.

Again, adherence to the rules is compatible with hate, because it can be motivated by pride and one-upmanship. It can be a means of cultivating superiority and a protection against compassionate action. For instance, there have been many who have looked on unemployment as being essentially due to the idleness and fecklessness of the unemployed. The castigation of sexual promiscuity has redounded on the heads of illegitimate children. The punishment of criminals has often been irrational because it expressed rage and vengeance.

All this is relevant to our view of free will. For, roughly since the time of Immanuel Kant, it has been not uncommon to view free will in a strictly individualistic way, in which the agent has a choice between right and wrong. This concept of free will tends to concentrate on the act of making a choice; it tends to neglect the real context of the choice. This context, however, is supremely important, in at least two ways.

First, moral action is not simply to do with summoning up the strength to fulfil one's duty; it is also a matter of discovering that duty. The adage that the way to hell is paved with good intentions rests on the perception that a limited and blind conception of duty is as fatal to human welfare as is the lack of a proper sense of duty. Thus the context of the exercise of the will is in the first instance the way in which we discover our duty. This may need imagination and sensitivity. These qualities are as important as determination. Thus the concentration of discussion of free will on the act of choice is not altogether satisfactory.

But secondly, we have to view the act of choice in a social context. Determination and imagination alike may be eroded in a society which has bad morale and a limited view. Because my values are so much shaped by the family and wider social institutions in which I have been brought up, my starting-point in the attempt to exercise imagination and determination is not chosen by me. Moreover, the process of liberation from blindness and prejudice is as likely to be sparked off by the imagination and example of others as it is to be set in train by myself. Even this is an understatement: moral insight is much more likely to arise from interplay between persons than it is to come unheralded from the lone individual. This is because in any event the concepts of morality are public ones, like the concepts of physics. They come through teaching and argument. Thus it may be more fruitful to ask, not so much whether the individual is free, but whether human society is. Does society itself have the capacity for novel insight and action? We shall revert to this topic shortly.

Thus the concept of "good works" must be expanded to include moral imagination. But this is not something we somehow choose. I cannot choose to be imaginative, just as I cannot choose to believe something (however much I sweat with conviction, I cannot bring myself to believe that there is an elephant in the room: there just isn't). However much I may screw up my determination, this will not bring the capacity and exercise of imagination. Again like faith and love, imagination is something which is awakened. We can indeed make choices which make this awakening more likely; we can choose to remove obstacles to it. But imagination itself is not directly of our choosing. In this respect, too, it is misleading to think of the overcoming of estrangement as being a matter of "good works" interpreted narrowly. In an important way, therefore, salvation is an educational rather than a behavioural task. It is a matter of

educing a certain vision, rather than of imposing behavioural conformity.

The preceding discussion of the nature of the human
predicament has been analytic, rather than historical. It has
been about the situation in which people find themselves,
rather than about the historical origins of their situation. It
will, as we pointed out earlier, be necessary to discuss those
origins, in view of the traditional concept of the Fall. But
there is a further piece of analysis which must be undertaken and which has been foreshadowed above. This is the
analysis of the nature of human freedom.

This problem has given rise to much discussion, both in
the religious and in the "secular" context. This discussion
has been especially prolix since the eighteenth century,
mainly because the rise of classical physics seemed to have
implications about freedom and determinism. The discussion has also been stimulated by the advances of biology
and psychology, for they brought with them an increased
awareness of the hereditary and unconscious determinants
of human behaviour. For the purposes of analysis it is possible to outline three main positions which philosophers
and others have taken up.

The first is that all human acts are determined by prior
causes. This view can be called "determinism". The reasons
advanced for it are as follows. First, classical physics seems
to imply that all natural events are determined by prior
causes: there is no special reason to except humanity from
this general principle. Second, as knowledge advances we
are increasingly knowledgeable about why humans behave
in certain ways. This suggests that ultimately we shall be
able to gain a full understanding of the mechanisms of
action. Third, and negatively, there is no point in claiming
that a free action is uncaused, for then it will be a random
event. Even in this case, the agent is not the determinant of
the action. Determinism in the above sense has usually involved a denial of human freedom: it being thought that

terms like "free" are, or ought to be, outmoded once we gain a fully scientific view of the world.

The second position is libertarianism, namely the view that some human acts (moral acts) are not determined by prior causes. The reasons advanced for this position are as follows. First, morality presupposes libertarianism. For "ought implies can". That is, if it is properly to be said that I ought to have met my aunt at the station, then it must have been possible for me to have done so. If I had been knocked down by a bus an hour before, or if I had been put in gaol, then it would be absurd to say that I ought to have been at the station. Ought, then, implies can. But if all my acts are determined by prior causes, I do not genuinely have a choice. If I choose to hit someone on the face, I can always argue that this act was in an important sense outside my control, since it was determined by earlier factors. Secondly, it is argued on behalf of libertarianism that since humans differ in such important ways from stones and moons and flowers—in being conscious, capable of thought and imagination and so forth—there is no special reason why a principle of determinism which applies to natural events should apply too to human beings.

The third main position is a variant of the first. It is a position which has been widely canvassed among British philosophers in the last twenty or thirty years. It is the view that there is a form of determinism which need not deny that some human acts are free. The argument is as follows. To say that one event causes another is to say that given the first you can in principle predict the second. Thus the thesis that all human acts are determined by prior causes boils down to this: that all human acts are in principle predictable. Of course we do not as yet know enough about human beings—perhaps we may never know enough—to be altogether effective in predicting future acts. But in principle (that is, given that one did have enough information and theoretical insight), it would be possible to predict any given human act. So determinism reduces to predictability. But now: to say that I can predict your action does not make that action any less free. For example, you go into a restaurant and I correctly predict that you will choose an omelette. Does that make your choice unfree? Were you forced by an evil management to take its omelette? Did the waiter hold a gun at you? Or do you have some irresistible omelette-compulsion? Do you find that whenever you are faced with an omelette you have a lunatic desire to wolf it down? The substance of the point being made is that as we ordinarily use terms like "free", they are opposed to others like "constrained" or "compulsive". A free act is one where there is a reasonable absence of internal (i.e. diseased psychological) and of external constraint. Thus the proponents of this view appeal to ordinary language in support of the thesis that free will is compatible with determinism. We can call this thesis "the compatibility thesis".

We have, then, three main positions which have been advanced: determinism, libertarianism and the compatibility thesis.

Though determinism has a nicely scientific air which commends it (and indeed, as we have seen, it arose in part at least from a consideration of the presuppositions of classical physics), it turns out not to be so very scientific. For firstly, it is unfalsifiable. Suppose I produce a supposed instance of an uncaused action, it is always open to the determinist to say: "It's just that we haven't found the cause yet." If, as was argued in an earlier chapter, a scientific theory has the hallmark of falsifiability, then determinism no longer counts as scientific. Second, modern science is not deterministic in the way Newtonian physics was. In subatomic physics, for instance, there are found to be theoretical limitations upon absolute prediction. This is not just a matter of the limited knowledge so far gained. It is a theoretical limitation, because (to put it crudely) observation itself disturbs, and necessarily disturbs, what is being observed. The theory itself entails that the future position and velocity of a particle cannot simultaneously be predicted. Probabilities and randomness thus enter into subatomic physics.

Nevertheless, as we have seen, this would not altogether help in regard to human phenomena. Suppose that an event in my brain, which is random and unpredictable, triggers off a moral act. Does this mean that I have freely chosen it? In any event, subatomic principles may not apply to human beings. With large objects (say brain-cells) the determinism of classical physics may apply. The random may here be irrelevant.

A more fruitful approach to the problem of free will may be had by combining criticisms which can be made against libertarianism and determinism respectively. Libertarianism concentrates on the supposed freedom of some *moral* acts. It is apparently in the moral sphere and that sphere alone that freedom can be found. It does not take much reflection to see what an unrealistic view this is. In deciding to run off with my neighbour's wife I am free; in deciding to put the other side into bat I am not. In deciding to steal my friend's watch, I am free; in deciding to invite someone to give a lecture I am not. Of course, the move can be made, and has been made, of saying that *all* acts are moral acts. There is always a moral issue, however small. But this blurs the important distinctions which we wish to make in speaking of something as a moral choice (as opposed to some other kind, such as aesthetic or tactical or political). The criticism, then, of a typical interpretation of libertarianism is that it divides up the human person: on the one hand a (free) moral agent, on the other a perhaps determined non-moral agent. The criticism is that the problems about human choice have been discussed in too narrow a context; the philosophical battle line has been drawn in the wrong place. In brief, if we are to make sense of freedom it must be something reaching far beyond the choice between doing one's moral duty and not. This point links up clearly enough with our earlier discussion of the need for moral (as well as other sorts of) imagination.

We can place this criticism of libertarianism alongside a major criticism of determinism. The latter doctrine supposes that all human events are in principle predictable. But this claim embodies not only an over-optimistic, but also a stereotyped, view of prediction. It is as though given the present conditions of a human being one could in principle predict his acts. But we must first take into account the role of other humans (not to mention natural events). Humans act in a dynamic situation of interplay with their fellows. Thus determinism, if it is to be applied to the individual, must also be able to work in society. But this is a tall order: for one can never guarantee in advance against novel insights and discoveries which may have profound social and individual effects. One cannot guarantee against new doctrines which inspire men to action. To put the matter crudely: the thesis of determinism implies that Marxism was predictable, that Relativity Theory was predictable, that Socrates' ethical teachings were predictable. But this is a paradox. It is a paradox because prediction itself involves a theory, a view of the world. To predict an earthquake in Chile one needs a theory about earthquakes. It is not enough to have counted past ones. One needs, then, a geological theory, as well as information about the structure of the Andes and what have you. If, then, predictions depend in part on theories, there can be no guarantee of their universal success, even in principle. For science itself is revisionary. Old theories are replaced by new: the progress of knowledge is dynamic and unstable. The theories, then, on which the prediction of human behaviour are or could be based are themselves liable to revision: and they surely cannot foresee this. A theory cannot solidly predict in detail its own demise. Thus there is an intrinsic difficulty about the deterministic hypothesis.

This criticism can be expanded by considering some particular examples. We are accustomed to think of the arts as creative, and the sciences are likewise creative. But what does creativity amount to? Impressionism, for instance, represented a new way of seeing the world, which though it cannot be fully understood except by reference to the previous state of painting, nevertheless added a new dimension to artistic experience and technique. Suppose we were to try in advance to anticipate Impressionism. What would we have to do? Either we could extrapolate from pre-Impressionistic ideas; or we could, so to say, paint in an Impressionist manner in pre-Impressionistic times to indicate the future. The former mode of prediction would fail, because Impressionism is not itself just a further development of pre-existent ideas, but contains something novel. The second mode of prediction is not so much prediction as anticipation. It is being an artist and creating something new. This itself would be unpredictable. Similarly, how could one on the basis of pre-Einstein physics predict the discovery of Relativity Theory? The same sort of argument as has been used about Impressionism applies here too. In brief, creativity in the arts and science is in a radical sense unpredictable, even in principle. It is not the case that there is no new thing under the sun, as determinism would imply. Ours is a universe which sometimes at least exhibits radical novelty.

To relate this to our earlier discussion of human qualities: the novelties which we find in the evolution of human ideas are a product of vision. This vision is not stereotyped, for if it were it would not have fruits. It is a vision which is creative: by transcending the past it brings something into being out of nothing.

If we combine this criticism of determinism with the former criticism of libertarianism we arrive at a sketch for the solution of the problems of determinism and free will. If determinism is the thesis that all human acts are predictable in principle, then it is false, because of the human capacity for radically novel vision. This vision can have profound moral and social effects. The new insights conveyed in Jesus' moral teaching, for instance, have had a widely diffused impact down the centuries. Hundreds of thousands of young physicists now learn Relativity Theory as a matter of course. Many people see the world differently because of the way Impressionists have painted. Thus new visions spread outward through society.

But also, and importantly, creativity and invention, though they involve transcending the past and transcending the social and cultural environment, do not involve the destruction of the past or of the environment. That is, we cannot understand creative novelty save in terms of the cultural world surrounding and preceding it. Shakespeare, for instance, has to be seen in the context of Elizabethan drama: this was the milieu in which he was able to exercise his remarkable gifts. Shakespeare in this sense is not timeless. Consequently, creativity is partly embedded in an existing culture. It cannot be separated from that. This is why it is partly misleading to speak of the individual's achievement: this achievement presupposes a social and cultural milieu, and the achievement, so to say, is also an achievement of society. (This is one reason why nations and traditions are proud of their great men. Thus the Church may go onward through its saints; but the saints likewise go onward through the Church.)

It is thus not absurd to see freedom as a property of human societies as well as of individuals. It is, as we suggested earlier, as appropriate to ask: Does human society have freedom? as it is to ask: Does the human being have freedom? The capacity for novel creativity, for new insights, is a feature of social existence.

The linking, then, of the notions of unpredictability and of the social dimension of freedom provides a solution to the problem of free will which avoids some of the pitfalls of the three theories described above. It avoids the suggestion implicit in determinism of a closed world where novelty is absent. It avoids the too individualistic and moralistic emphasis of typical libertarianism: for it sees freedom in relation to human imagination as a whole, and in the context of society. It avoids the unambitious platitudinousness implicit in the compatibility thesis, for it goes beyond the idea of a negative freedom which consists in absence of constraint, internal or external. The unease which men feel about determinism, and therefore about the compatibility thesis, arises, I think, from the obscure feeling that positive breaks with the past are possible, however stereotyped our imaginations and characters may be. This feeling is correct: for the inspiration of new moral or other insight is always possible in a dynamic society.

But we have been unduly harsh on the compatibility thesis in one respect. For it has the merit of pointing to the conditions under which we excuse people from blame, and under which ordinary control is possible. We must in practice make use of the ordinary idea of freedom in teaching skills and controls. Nevertheless, it is also necessary to see that human and social creativity can at any time bring a conversion—a transformation either of the individual or of the possibilities available to him—which will translate his skills and controls into a new sphere.

What we may call the "social creativity" theory of freedom is relevant to the idea of blame. On the typical libertarian view of free will, the individual can be seen as totally responsible for his moral acts. If, then, he acts wrongly, he can justly be blamed. On the determinist view, blame is strictly out of place except as a means of engineering good conduct. It helps to induce shame, which will influence action. The former account is, I would argue, unrealistic: the latter is paradoxical. The former is unrealistic because men are and cannot be lone heroes. The latter is paradoxical, for I can feel no shame if blame is strictly inapplicable to my actions. Or rather, if I do feel shame, I am irrational.

The social creativity theory, however, must present a somewhat different solution, though this will incorporate something of the spirit of the deterministic account. The merit of the latter account is that it leads us away from what may be termed the "gossipy" view of moral judgments. We very often get into the habit of trying to give ourselves and our neighbours moral marks. "So-and-so is a bad man," we aver, sitting back as though something important has been said. But what after all is the point of such grading? What, more importantly, is the point of moral language? Surely moral language is practical: it is ultimately to do with changing life. It is concerned with diminishing evil and preparing the good. It is concerned with changing people. The gossipy approach has two defects, then. It is moral language idling (and it is usually people idling); and induces in folk the notion that moral esteem is more important than moral caring. The deterministic theory, by ascribing to praise and blame a frankly engineering function—the function of changing people who can be changed thereby—does not fall into the trap of the gossip. Nevertheless, it has the paradoxical irrationality to which I alluded earlier.

If we bear in mind that the individual agent is not a lone hero and that the main point of moral discourse is to change the world for the better, we can begin to find a solution. If we take the social dimension of freedom seriously, we begin to recognise that we participate in one another's actions. Thus the spirit of "blame" is better expressed by saying "It is a pity that one of us did that", rather than by saying "*You* should not have done that". The aim of moral judgment cannot be a hostile and derogatory one if we genuinely feel solidarity with the wrong-doer. The story of Jesus and the woman taken in adultery points to this. Moral judgments then should be undertaken for a sort of engineering purpose, but not quite the one envisaged by the deterministic theory.

The engineering purpose of moral judgments should be this: to help in the creation of conversion—to help in the creation of a new insight. The engineering involved is therefore itself part of the social process in which men can be liberated from the unsatisfactory trammels of the past. Moral judgment itself is an element in the production of freedom.

But, it will be said, all this is not particularly realistic to

the situation in which actual moral education takes place.
Do we not bring up children to behave ethically through
teaching them about good men and bad men? Do we not
continually imply a gossipy, grading view of moral judgment? Do we not also categorically describe some actions
as good and others as naughty? Yes, we do these things;
but two comments are in order. First, does the parent who
castigates his child as naughty take this judgment seriously?
Does he set himself over against the child in judgment?
Does he not rather say this thing because it will help the
child (or he thinks it will)? Does he not use such judgments
in the very context of which we have spoken above—the
context of solidarity? It is perhaps not easy for the child to
see this: and parents sometimes are hostile rather than
loving. But the case of the loving parent bears out an engineering account, and one which makes sense of solidarity.

Secondly, the ways in which children are introduced to
morality are necessarily restricted by the child's understanding. Rules are taught and understood as "absolute" at an
early stage. The child does not yet appreciate that exceptions may be made or the rules altered. He does not yet
arrive at a position where he can legislate for himself. And
in moral judgment too the child's understanding has to be
nurtured by instances of heroism and villainy. His ideals
may still be crude, but they are beginning to be formed.
The transition to an adult point of view—or rather the
transition to real insight, for adults often enough stay at the
child's level—involves a revision of what has previously
been learned. Consequently, we do not need to take as our
standard the child's initial understanding of moral judgment.

Something of this process of transition can be seen historically in the Old Testament, and more clearly still in
the New, we can observe the transition from the treatment
of the law in a tabu-like way to a perception of the spirit
which ought to inform the law. Here the Incarnation is of
peculiar importance. A tabu-like law and the conception of
moral judgment as a means of grading people can easily

give rise, in the context of theism, to a belief in a God who is over against and hostile to his children: one who lays down rigid rules and punishes those who fail to obey them. Such a feeling sometimes comes upon us in reading the Old Testament (and it was a conception which St Paul, despite his revolutionary conversion, with difficulty overthrew). It is true that this feeling involves a distortion of the main Old Testament view (Israel was, after all, the Chosen People). But the feeling is there, and reflects some of our present anxieties about God and about men's estimate of us. But the feeling fades when we contemplate the meaning of the Incarnation. For here God becomes involved and entangled in the process of the human striving for vision and love. He is not, as it were, outside the process, passing judgment upon it. He is within it, trying to induce the insights and the loyalties which will give point to moral language. The saying "Father, forgive them: for they know not what they do" is a recognition that in part this attempt to stimulate insight and love had failed. It is also an expression of the uselessness of condemnation. Jesus oddly too seems to have repudiated the title "good". This is puzzling on the gossipy, grading theory. It makes sense when we see moral judgment in the context of participation in one another's actions.

The social creativity theory, moreover, makes more sense of modern advances in psychology and biology than does typical libertarianism. We need not be frightened or anxious for our theory because it has been shown that some of our actions and attitudes have their roots in the unconscious. We need not be other than excited by psycho-analytical theory (even if its claims often outrun its achievements). We can appreciate these developments in understanding for two reasons. First—and this is profoundly the more important reason—new understanding can cure people. It can help to liberate them from irrational and painful impulses. It can bring light to minds that have become overshadowed by the past. New knowledge is new power. It is interesting in this connection that classical psycho-analysis, as propounded by Freud, so strongly holds that self-understanding is a crucial part in cure. There is a moral here: that insight is often more important than will-power. This is in line with the whole emphasis of the social creativity theory of freedom. In religious terms, faith is more important than works. Secondly, it should be noted that the growth of psychiatry has been accompanied by a strong disapproval of judgmental attitudes. It is central to the view of most psychiatrists that the gossipy, grading theory of moral judgment is harmful, and indeed obsolete. This is partly because psychiatry involves co-operation between doctor and patient, and increasingly between patient and patient. The attitude is of a solidarity in which men are partners in the pursuit of health. These attitudes help to reinforce the participatory theory of moral judgment which we deduced from the social creativity theory of freedom. They give a new insight, moreover, into demands for forgiveness and into the injunction "Judge not that ye be not judged". (But the latter injunction can so easily be twisted: it can so easily become: "You people who go around judging others are a crowd of sinners." Or it can have an even more sinister flavour: "You stuck-up people—just you wait.")

The social creativity theory can now be related to our earlier conclusions about the human predicament and about salvation from estrangement. The human predicament involves, as we argued, a situation where the human qualities of vision and love are so much blocked by blindness and hate. Though we can be co-workers with the Creator in the process of creation, we are implicated so often in destructiveness and social lethargy. We feel frustrated and ineffective, partly because the individual is under pressure from social forces which he cannot control, and partly because a new effectiveness depends on a conversion, on a vision and love which we seek but do not have. There is no recipe, however, for vision and love. They have to arise. The best we can do is to seek, by widening our interests and sympathies, and by nurturing the limited good which we already see. On the social creativity theory, vision and love do arise here and there, in creative unpredictability, and we can participate in their opportunities and blessings. From there we can build anew. Thus the human predicament is one in which there is both despair and hope: despair because we cannot create vision and love to order: they come through conversions, through new insights: hope because such conversions happen, and can be widely diffused.

Part of the meaning of salvation was found earlier in the creation of the new society in which men can be effective co-workers with God. The social creativity theory of human freedom can give added point to this conception. For the very creativity of Jesus represents a breakthrough in human freedom. It means a new liberation, through the diffusion of his insight, and through the intimate participation in the divine life which God's self-revelation in Christ has made possible. Thus we can see the life of Christ as imparting a new dynamic to human society. Part of human freedom is divine freedom.

The social creativity theory, moreover, can cast some more light on the relation between faith and works. For the vision and love which breakthroughs in vision and love can impart to the individual are of the nature of faith. They involve a response which fires the individual, not just an external conformity to that for which a man has no heart. Doing one's duty is important, but it can be soul-destroying when it is not believed in.

It is now time to review these arguments against an historical background. What do these arguments imply in regard to the traditional picture of the Fall? Already, we have noted that Adam stands for mankind, so that one dimension of the Fall story can be explained as this—that in a strong sense we men share in each other's predicament. It is not just that you and I and George and President Johnson individually have similar frustrations and defects. It is rather that our individual frustrations and defects are mutually interdependent or overlapping. Such interdependence is, so to say, reinforced if we adopt a participatory attitude to human evil. This is a moral ideal of interdependence: the ideal that we use "we" when talking of mankind.

But of course the Fall story also tries to give some kind of account of how evil came into the world. The usual Christian interpretation has to lay the blame chiefly on mankind. This interpretation is partly determined by the need to do something about the so-called problem of evil. If God is good, how is it that his creation displays evil? It cannot be God's doing, or he would not be good. At a later point in this book it will be necessary to enter into a fuller discussion of this old, yet also for all that harrowing, problem.

A careful reading of *Genesis*, however, does not justify us in thinking that the writer intended the story of Adam to explain only the origin of evil. The whole mysterious account of the tree of life has a subtler meaning, and one which is echoed by Babylonian and Sumerian myths. The difficulty over Adam's eating of the tree of good and evil is expressed in 3.22: " 'Behold, the man has become like one of us, knowing good and evil; and now, lest he put forth his hand and take also of the tree of life, and eat, and live for ever'—therefore the Lord God sent him forth from the garden of Eden . . ."

This account implies two things: first, that the knowledge of good and evil is a God-like property; and second that God was jealous of the possibility of man's grasping divine immortality through his own initiative. This latter point, taken out of the mythological context in which it is found, could be puzzling. Why should God be worried? Why should he be mean enough to deprive man of such a blessing?

The sentiment which the story expresses is this. By his own nature, God possesses immortality. If such immortality is ever to be given to man, it must be given. Conversely, it is pride and *hybris* for man to grasp at the divine essence. Man seeks to force his way into heaven, by force or trickery. Behind the myth, there lies the sense that God and man are separated by a great gulf. On the one hand is the splendour and holiness of the Creator; on the other hand the weakness and ambition of man. The ambition, however, to be God is misplaced—not to say blasphemous. To be a co-worker with the Creator—yes, this is possible; to seek equality with God is false and absurd.

The knowledge of good and evil, however, already represents an invasion of the divine domain, according to the *Genesis* account. Already Adam is "like one of us". As a consequence, Adam's work becomes toil; and his existence is hedged in by death.

It is somewhat naïve to take the *Genesis* poem so literally that it is interpreted as meaning that before the events described in it man was free from death. In any case, immortality was that which God feared he might yet grasp through eating of the tree of life. The myth is not about some catastrophic change which occurred to prehistoric man's condition. Rather it is a portrayal of the consequences of the knowledge of good and evil. This knowledge itself presupposes both vision and love. Without a glimpse of these, there cannot be appreciation of the nature of evil. But the vision and the love of which men somehow became capable themselves highlight the blindness and hate. In the awareness of his powers, man can no longer see himself as part of nature. He is no longer unconsciously merged with the trees and antelopes. He no longer lives the life of animal sport and clawing. He is no longer part of the landscape. He begins to stand back from the landscape. He begins to withdraw from the unconscious waking of brute life. Having the conscious power to change life, he thereby becomes haunted by the limits of change, by death. He becomes haunted by death because it is consciousness which confers meaning and value on his pleasures and pains and successes. Death is the finishing of consciousness, and the route by which alone man can merge back into unconcious nature. The threat of death, then, haunts men, once they have achieved detachment from the natural background. Through the knowledge of good and evil—through man's very acquirement of this divine capacity—man's life becomes overshadowed by grim mortality.

The power, too, is double-edged. It gives men creativity and the chance to destroy. It nurtures love but it generates hate. It is not long in the *Genesis* story before the murderous Cain appears on the scene. In the awareness of this power of evil, and in the awareness of his finitude, man feels estranged from his vision of the good. He, if he recognises a Creator, also recognises that somehow he has become alienated from that Creator. Indeed, just as his self-awareness brings him into detachment from nature, so that his world now seems alien, likewise he is detached from the Creator of nature, so that God seems alien. This is the price of knowledge: it is the price of the ascent towards his own power and fulfilment. In these respects, there seems to be a fall away from God. But also there is an ascent.

The Christian tradition has often concentrated rather a lot upon the black side of this picture. The idea of inherited sin made it seem as though a taint was handed down through the generations. This concentration, however, on the darker side is not altogether warranted by the myth; nor has the Jewish tradition placed such an emphasis on the taintedness of mankind. But of course it is reasonable to recognise that the estranged predicament of men is continuous with the past: there is a social inheritance of evil. In this sense, the doctrine of original sin is meaningful. But it is also necessary to recognise that the "Fall" was also a moment of self-awareness and opportunity.

Modern knowledge, though still fragmentary, can illuminate the problem: for we see that prehistoric men emerged dimly from an animal ancestry. We can see that the emergence of conscious life was the result of an exceedingly long and complex interplay of biological forces. We are therefore no longer content with a myth which presents the creation of man as though mankind came fully-fledged into the world. The *Genesis* myth, of course—and as has been repeatedly stressed here—is not in its conception an attempt at scientific explanation. Nevertheless, its language and its presuppositions are liable to conflict with our language and our presuppositions. We may extract its religious and moral message; but we also want a myth of our own. We also want an account which places man's emergence firmly in the context of the evolutionary process.

Nevertheless, the account given above, of the consequences of self-awareness—of the consequences of the knowledge of good and evil—in no way conflicts with the evolutionary picture. It is a kind of reconstruction of the results of the at first dim capacities of men to stand back from the world in which they found themselves. We do not, of course, have enough evidence to reconstruct in detail the life of the earliest men. But it is probable that very early men had a mythological framework for interpreting their world. Already a vision of something beyond the immediate environment and a ritual concern for death indicated something of the process of alienation from nature.

Though an evolutionary picture of mankind's emergence out of an animal background is unfavourable to a literal interpretation of *Genesis*, it is in another way favourable to the Biblical picture as a whole. For the Biblical narrative stresses above all the historical unfolding of God's purpose. This historical process is directional. It is not the repetition of the past, but the supervening of new occurrences upon that past. Similarly, evolution, though it did not for an immense period produce the human consciousness which is a necessary part of that which is properly called history, has a directional aspect. This is not to say that the biologist, by an examination of the past, can detect a purpose in the evolutionary process. As we said earlier, the notion of purpose no longer seems fruitful in biology. Thus evolution is not directional in the sense of displaying an inner purpose driving towards some higher goal (though there have not been lacking philosophers and biologists who have seen

evolution in this way—in recent times, the notorious Teilhard de Chardin). But evolution is directional in the sense
that there is an unfolding of novelty: later stages are different from earlier ones: more complex and subtle organisms
replace or supervene upon the simpler: a world once slimy
and vegetable becomes a world replete with monkeys and
shellfish. It is therefore difficult not to think of the evolutionary process as a kind of history: it is not yet human
history, but it is somewhat similarly directional. Thus the
essence of the Biblical picture still remains: the thought
that the evolutionary creativity of God merges impercept-
ibly into the history of mankind.

A consequence, however, of this picture is that it is not
possible or realistic to look back to an early golden age.
The garden of Eden has sometimes been seen as a prehistoric paradise from which alas men have been driven.
There was no early paradise, unless we count a total merging with nature as a kind of heaven (it was hellish too, no
doubt). Our ancestors were not better than us, living in
blissful communion with God. It is doubtful whether they
had a clear idea of God. It is virtually certain that their life
was often nasty, usually short and sometimes brutish. It
was a life of hunting and grubbing and cowering from
thunderstorms. It was a life of lizards and snakes and sup-
purating scratches. It was a life in societies, but societies
which often collided. It was a dirty, hairy life. Yet it contained, we may presume, the seeds of vision and love—the
seeds which were later to flower more splendidly. From this
point of view, the traditional picture of a primeval Fall
seems like a fairy story. It does seem so, though we can
still recognise the way in which the story expresses the
contemporary predicament of the writer.

The fading of a romantic picture of a golden age of
Adam means that we can no longer see Christ's work as
being a kind of cure of the disease which since has inflicted
mankind. Christ's work is not strictly the restoration of a
primeval *status quo*. It is no longer easy to think in the

terms used by the hymn . . . "a second Adam to the fight and to the rescue came". But in any event it is scarcely true to the New Testament or to the testimony of the early Church to suppose that Christ's work is merely restorative —as though something had gone wrong which the master-doctor now puts right. Christ is higher than Adam. He is the Creator continuing his work. He brings something positive and new into human history. He may cure men's estrangement, but it is through leading men higher: it is not through returning man to a supposed primitive condition. He brings eternal life, but a life that was not held, then lost, by Adam. The evolutionary picture, then, will serve to highlight the positive novelty of Christ and the achievements of Israel. And if the past direction can be seen as pointing onwards to Christ, so Christ points onward into the future. The evolutionary picture, in brief, brings out the dynamic quality of revelation and of the new society.

The whole of the preceding argument is, as was said earlier, merely an attempt to stimulate thought. It presents one picture of salvation, estrangement, freedom and man's origins. It would be idle and arrogant to think that it is the only feasible (if indeed it is a feasible) account. But it is an attempt to be realistic about the human predicament, and to see the latter in relation to the Biblical material. I remain convinced that this is the right way round. It is not educationally satisfactory to impose the categories of the Bible on the world around us, but rather we should let the world around us speak for itself. Then there is hope that we can see the relevance of the Biblical message to our world. If we work the other way round, there is a danger that we shall be looking at our world through double spectacles— through the spectacles of ancient writers, and through the spectacles we use to look at the spectacles of these ancient writers. In the process we can be mistaken not only about the import of the Bible but about our own world. We can create a phantasy religious world which does not correspond to our real environment. It would be no wonder if the young were disillusioned with the results.

We may sum up the results of this chapter briefly as follows. First, estrangement has to be seen in the context of the qualities of vision and love of which human beings are capable. Such vision and love reflect the creative and loving nature of God. Thus the cure for estrangement brings out the way in which men can be fully co-workers with the Creator. Second, the saving work of Christ partly consists in the creation of the new society in which the triumph of the creative process is assured, and through which men can have a direct and intimate relationship with God. Thus Christ's incarnation represents a new dimension in the process of God's self-introduction (his revelation) to mankind. Third, human freedom has a direct connection with the qualities of vision and love. Freedom is a social phenomenon in which unpredictable creativity can become diffused through society. Consequently, the old opposition between determinism and libertarianism is outmoded. Determinism is right in pointing to an engineering concept of moral judgment and in stressing the degree to which we are moulded by circumstance: libertarianism is right in its intuition that the world of human action is not a closed world, but one which is open to novel possibilities. The theory of social creativity allows for both these insights, and points to a moral attitude where we participate in the actions of others. Fourth, the theory of free will is relevant to the doctrine of salvation, because it stresses the importance of inspiration and "conversion" rather than just the adherence to a preconceived system of duties, and also because its recognition of the social dimension chimes in with the idea of the new society founded by Christ. Fifth, the social nature of estrangement gives a certain meaning to traditional ideas of inherited sin; but we must also recognise the evolutionary character of the emergence of man. Consequently, the Fall is also—through the knowledge of good and evil—a kind of ascent. Though man feels estranged from the Creator he has also glimpsed the vision and the love which give him the capacity to be a creative process. In turn, Christ's work is seen as essentially the injection of something new into human history, not just a restoration of an illusory past golden age.

These, then, are some of the ideas presented in this chapter. But already there will be questions about human history. Have we not treated it very much as centring on Israel and Christ? We have not yet raised the problems presented by the existence of important and noble religious traditions outside the Judeo-Christian one. We have been expounding a version of Christianity. But why Christianity?

CHAPTER FIVE

CHRISTIANITY AND OTHER FAITHS

Our contemporaries, and especially young people, are increasingly aware of the existence of other faiths. There was a time, due to the cultural tribalism of Europe and the narrow syllabuses of school history, when civilisation and enlightenment tended to be identified with Europe and Christianity. Warships, administrators and missionaries tended to carry this message to the worlds of Asia and Africa. Fortunately, however, we live in more enlightened times. It is no longer easy to think in the old way. It is now clear, as it should always have been clear, that the nobilities of other faiths are not lightly to be neglected and despised.

This interest in other faiths centres chiefly in Indian religion—Hinduism and, above all, Buddhism (Buddhism arose in India, though of course it is virtually absent now from its homeland—mirroring the situation of Christianity in relation to Palestine). The reasons for the special interest in Indian religions are not far to seek. First, Judaism and Islam, for all their differences from Christianity, belong to the same religious world: their heritages overlap greatly. They preach a monotheism founded on that of the Old Testament. Indian religions look very different. Buddhism, for instance, does not require belief in a Creator. Theravada Buddhism, as found in Ceylon, Burma and parts of South-East Asia, is agnostic about such a Being, while only in a limited way are certain phases of the Mahayana (Greater Vehicle) like Christian theism. Thus Indian religions gain part of their fascination from their very difference from Christianity. This confers on them a certain freshness, which is important in an age when many people in the West are alienated from, and somewhat hostile to, ecclesiastical traditions. For Buddhism and Hinduism represent religious alternatives not entangled with a suspect past.

Second, Indian religions stand out in people's interest because of the fading of the alternatives. The Taoism of ancient China never became missionary beyond the bounds of Chinese culture, and fell into a long and magical decay. Confucianism is more relevant to China than to societies in the West, and in any case is being submerged by Marxism in mainland China. Shintoism and the tribal or national religions of Africa do not have a universal appeal, and are adversely affected by modern social and political developments. Judaism is essentially a closed faith, while Islam's basic fundamentalism gives it little attraction to the Western sceptic who yet seeks faith. It is not, therefore, unnatural for a modern Hinduism and Buddhism to stand out as live options.

Third, there are, of course, the inherent attractions of Buddhist and Hindu thought and practice. To these we shall come anon.

This new climate of opinion about the "non-Christian" religions (though we could equally classify Christianity and Hinduism as "non-Buddhist"—the old cultural tribalism still lingers on)—this new climate of opinion means that people are not altogether content to be taught "religion" as though it is coterminous with the Judeo-Christian tradition. This is so for two reasons. First, the teaching of religion is informative—it tells people about the religious aspects of human culture. If, then, we are concerned with an understanding of human culture, we should in some degree at least be concerned with all the major religions. Second, apart from the informative content of the teaching of religion, there is the problem of the truth of religion. Naturally, people will be deeply concerned with this issue. But once we note that impressive and noble religious traditions appear to preach conflicting doctrines, we will want to know how we arrive at the truth between them. More particularly, it will be insufficient to make a simple appeal to one revelation, for it is an obvious question to ask: "But why that revelation?"

The present chapter is chiefly concerned with this last question—the problem of truth in a multi-religious world. But it needs to be stressed with all possible clarity that the apologetic task of defending Christianity should in no wise creep into the historical presentation of other faiths. This is a fault found in a number of books on the comparative study of religion. To mix up historical analysis and religious apologetic is foolish, uncandid and self-defeating. It is foolish, because it fails to bring out the proper flavour of other faiths—of why they appeal to their adherents. It is uncandid because it smuggles argument into what should be sympathetic description. It is self-defeating, because prejudice is easily detected and is usually interpreted as a sign of weakness. Thus it needs strongly to be stressed that the teaching of religion should attempt to move from inside other traditions: it should not seek to foist a Christian (or what have you) interpretation upon other faiths.

However, the intent of the present chapter is not to present a brief history of other faiths. In any event the space is too limited for such a giant task. Rather the aim is to consider some of the apologetic and doctrinal arguments which arise out of the confrontation between the great faiths. Partly for the reasons mentioned earlier, the main concentration will be upon the intellectual interplay between Christianity on the one hand and Hinduism and Buddhism on the other. This is not to deny the great achievements of Jewish, Islamic, Chinese and African culture. It is only to make a selection from within the complex dialogue of religions in accordance with the main interests of Westerners today.

Two initial reactions to the multiplicity of faiths are natural. One is to say: "They are none of them true: see how the great teachers disagree." Another is to say: "They are all great teachers, great traditions: they must all somehow point to the same truth." The first reaction is altogether too cavalier, and it is worth countering it with the question: "What theory of inspiration or insight do you have which would lead you to expect all the great teachers to say the same thing?"

The second reaction, which we can call "pan-religionism", has received impetus in modern times through its advocacy by a number of prominent Hindu thinkers. It is indeed part of the ideology of modern Hinduism that all religions point to the same truth. This is partly because Hinduism rightly prides itself on its tolerance. It is partly too because the theory makes sense of the internal structure of Hinduism, where widely differing beliefs about God and the Absolute at different levels of sophistication have and are held by different elements in Hindu society. Thus the unity of Hinduism itself is predicated on a theory which points too to the unity of all religions.

There is an obvious difficulty with pan-religionism, namely that the various faiths indeed seem to preach different doctrines. How can Theravada Buddhist agnosticism be reconciled with Christian theism? How can the personal theism of Ramanuja be squared with the doctrine of a nonpersonal Absolute as expressed by Shankara? How can the Islamic belief in the eternity of the Koran square with Christian beliefs about the Bible? How can the Indian belief in reincarnation be reconciled with the Judeo-Christian account of resurrection and immortality? Obviously, then, there are divergences of overt teaching.

At least two ripostes to this objection can be made from the side of neo-Hindu pan-religionism. One riposte is to refuse to identify Truth with propositions. The doctrines are only signposts along the way to the experience of the Truth. The Truth itself cannot be formulated. The other riposte is to say that different doctrines represent different *levels* of religious truth. Some concern a personal God who is worshipped by the ordinary man; others concern a higher non-personal Absolute with which the mystic can realise his identity. The number of levels can be multiplied, and the contradictions between doctrines eliminated by assigning different doctrines to different levels of truth. Thus the idea of a personal Creator is valid at its own level; but not at a higher level—and so on.

The first riposte—the non-propositional one—has a strong appeal, partly because, as we saw in an earlier chapter, there are reasons for looking on revelation as the self-manifestation of the divine Being rather than as a set of propositions. Also, we are sensitive to the depths of meaning which religious language has, and the imposition of doctrinal formulae sometimes thus seems wooden and misleading. Further, we are aware that there is indeed something ineffable about ultimate reality: it is a commonplace of religion that words are inadequate to the task of expressing fully the nature of the Godhead, or of nirvana, etc. Thus it seems plausible to hold that the Truth to which different doctrines point cannot be formulated. Finally, we see the force of the old Eastern saying, that doctrines are like a finger pointing at the moon. The man who concentrates on the doctrines, to the exclusion of what they point to, is like a person who looks at the pointing finger instead of looking at the moon.

Nevertheless, correct as some or all these observations may be, there remains a difficulty in the "non-propositional" riposte. We can put the point most strongly in the following way. Suppose that God is *totally* indescribable—that there is *nothing* that can be properly said about him—then why call him God? The very use of the term implies some conception of his nature: it implies something in the way of belief and doctrine. It is thus a contradiction to speak of a totally indescribable God. We could still perhaps speak of a totally indescribable Truth: an utterly unknown X. But why should this X be connected with religion rather than with atheism? Why should it be attainable along one way rather than another? Why indeed should we bother with it at all? The notion that the Truth then is totally indescribable is self-defeating. It cannot be a view which is relevant to the religious quest. But then on the other hand if our words about God and the Absolute, about Christ and nirvana, are in some degree appropriate—even though they may not be adequate to the full expression of these realities —if this is so, then we are back with the problem that the words in different religions do say different things. True enough, the differences are exaggerated often; and there is no doubt that we are too often victims of a superficial interpretation of religious belief. But even so it will be recognised by the pious Christian and the pious Buddhist that their aims are divergent and that the flavours of the two faiths are unmistakably different. Thus ultimately the first riposte—the "non-propositional" one—breaks down.

But before moving to consider the second, we should note a feature of the "non-propositional" riposte: we should note its inner dynamic. The reason why it is appealing, and the reason why it has a strong hold in neo-Hindu apologetics as well as in some expositions of Zen Buddhism, is that it chimes in with an important aspect of mystical experience. It happens that the interior quest (the kind of quest which in Christianity was undertaken by Eckhart, St John of the Cross, Boehme and other famous contemplatives) is central to Buddhism and is prominent in the Hindu way of life. It also happens that there is an increased interest in it among educated Westerners today. Yoga, mainstream Buddhism and Zen all have their attractions in the West. And it also happens—and here we come to the important aspect of mysticism mentioned above—that the mystical experience itself is in a certain sense ineffable or indescribable. It does not involve mental images or dreamlike visions: in the mystical state, the contemplative has no outer perceptions. Nor does he go on thinking in the typical sense of the term. He is wrapped in a "cloud of unknowing". He is beyond perceptions and concepts. Consequently, much ordinary language which we use to describe perceptions and thoughts does not apply. This ineffability accounts for the fact that the contemplative thinks of his experience as contact or merging with an indescribable Something, an unutterable Truth, an indefinable State. This is the religious root of the idea that ultimate Reality is "beyond words". This, then, helps to give a religious appeal to the non-propositional riposte. Nevertheless, it is worth remarking that as a matter of fact also the contemplative typically sees his unutterable experience in the context of a certain Path and a certain set of doctrines. The Buddhist identifies it with the attainment of nirvana (and Buddhism has a whole doctrine of nirvana); the Christian sees it as union with the Godhead or as the consummation of the spiritual marriage of the soul with God; the Muslim sees it likewise; the Hindu sees it in various ways, according to the different theologies contained within the Hindu system; and so on. These interpretations of the experience take the mystic beyond the unutterable to at least a limited description of the nature of his vision.

The second riposte—the one which pigeon-holes doctrines at different levels of religious truth—is open to criticism also, because it is both hard to work and uncritical in its assumptions. It is hard to work because some doctrines plainly conflict which equally plainly belong to the same level. For instance, the doctrine of reincarnation is plainly about man (and other living beings); the Muslim doctrine of judgment and the after-life is also plainly about the destiny of man. The Muslim doctrine denies reincarnation; Hinduism affirms it. Is it or is it not the case that when I die I shall be reborn in some living form? It is hard to see how a conflict between teachings can be avoided here. Again, the organic nature of religions and of systems of doctrine, to which we alluded in an earlier chapter, means that there are subtle differences in ideas which are superficially alike. Thus the conceptions of God in Christianity, Islam and

Hinduism have certain differences, precisely because of the differences in the whole patterns of belief in these faiths.

The many-level theory is not merely difficult to work. It is also, as we have remarked, uncritical in its assumptions. It assumes that conflicts can be eradicated by a given scheme of levels of truth. It forgets that the scheme itself may come under criticism: it forgets that the scheme itself may be unacceptable to a given religious tradition. It forgets that there can be alternative schemes of levels of truth.

For example, it is common enough for liberal-minded Christians to attempt to give an interpretation of other religions which attempts to make sense of them in terms of the Christian revelation. Thus Professor R. C. Zaehner, the highly distinguished Roman Catholic scholar who occupies the Spalding Chair of Eastern Religions and Ethics at Oxford, has, in a number of works, undertaken this task. One of the problems one has to deal with is to give an account of non-theistic mysticism. In Buddhism and in classical Yoga, for instance, the "liberation" which mystical experience brings is not interpreted in terms of union with God or anything of that sort. But are we to write off all this treasury of experience and holy living? Are we to dismiss as useless and misguided these great traditions? Professor Zaehner certainly recoils from this "solution". Instead, he has a double-decker view of mystical experience. First, there is the level where the mystic realises the essential identity of his own soul. This soul-mysticism is possible through natural efforts. Second, at a higher level there is the mysticism of the love of God in which the contemplative attains, through the grace of God (and thus not just naturally), a kind of union with the divine Being.

This account is not, however, acceptable to the typical neo-Hindu apologist, who if anything wants to reverse the levels. He sees the attainment of the Self as being the higher stage; the love of God is at a lower level, useful though it may be in cultivating the qualities which will bring a person to the higher Truth. The Hindu is thus Zaehner upside down.

Again, there are those who would reject the idea of levels. Ramanuja, for instance, the great medieval Hindu theist, strongly attacked the idea. From this point of view, the different "levels" become essentially incompatible. Thus there are four main positions which can be taken up in regard to two levels or supposed levels. They can be arranged in the order AB (as with Zaehner); or in the order BA (like the neo-Hindu); or they can occur as A but not B, or as B but not A. In concrete terms, one can have different arrangements of two elements: the religion of devotion to a personal God and the religion of the contemplative realisation of a Self or Absolute. One can count the former as higher (Zaehner). One can count the latter as higher (Hindu monism). One can count the former but exclude the latter (Protestantism, for instance, typically takes this form). Or one can count the latter but exclude the former (agnostic Buddhism, classical Yoga and Jainism all do this).

Yet the four positions do not exhaust the possibilities. It is also open to us to say that contemplative mysticism if correctly interpreted is strongly compatible with devotional theism. We can say that what the mystic finds within is the God that the worshipper finds without. This is the typical position of theistic mystics, such as St John of the Cross and the Muslim and Jewish mystics. This position involves the thesis that the mysticism of the Self or Absolute is not essentially different from theistic mysticism: it is only that there is a diversity of doctrinal interpretation—it is only that the "vision" is fitted into a different frame of reference. Thus, on this view, the Buddha in his Enlightenment saw what St John of the Cross saw; but because the Buddha was disillusioned with the beginnings of theism to be discovered in his environment he did not proffer a theistic interpretation of his vision. We can call this fifth position the "synthetic" one. It involves neither the ordering AB nor the ordering BA, but the equality between A and B.

Consequently, the questions which occur about the difference in doctrines as between the great religions cannot be solved by the many-level theory. For the same sort of questions will recur when we try to decide on the various alternatives outlined above. Both Hindu and Christian apologists are inclined to forget this dimension of the problem.

We can put that problem in another way by asking what the nature of *dialogue* between religions amounts to. As a preliminary, of course, dialogue means elucidating one another's basic positions. It means thus far the interchange of teaching and insight. But dialogue is not just this. Nor is it dogmatic preaching. The presupposition of dialogue is that there is real listening, and a real willingness to engage together in a common search for truth. But what do these last requirements themselves amount to? Surely they mean this: that wherever it is possible there should be the employment of common criteria of truth. It is not enough to establish Christianity on the basis of some test of truth which itself presupposes the truth of Christianity. To take a crude example: we cannot just say that Christianity is true because the Church says that it is true; for the authority of the Church itself depends on the truth of Christianity. We must not, then, be circular. Circularity, as well as being logically shame-making, conduces to preaching at the other religionist. "We say this, because we say this, because we say this .." The circular droning of preaching here is not part of a real dialogue. If, then, dialogue means that we must search for the truth together, by common criteria—so far as these can be discovered (for the criteria of truth in religion are not so easily come by)—it is not enough to solve the problem of conflict by imposing an apologetic multi-level scheme of doctrine. It is not enough to start from Christian or Hindu premisses and categorise other faiths through them.

Let me not be misunderstood. I would not deny that it is important for, say, the Christian thinker to understand Hindu or Buddhist history and experience in terms of his

own theology and experience. If we believe at all in theology, we believe in a doctrine of history. If we believe in a
doctrine of history we believe in a doctrine of Indian history. We may wish to discover the modes under which God
has revealed himself in that history. All this is a justifiable
(indeed unavoidable) theological enterprise, and we shall
later attempt a sketch of this very thing. But in the context
of dialogue and of the truth of religion, it is not a fundamental enterprise. The Christian interpretation of Buddhism
or Hinduism or Islam itself depends on the truth of Christianity. We cannot decide upon it without a prior decision
for Christianity. It is this more fundamental question which
dialogue is concerned with. It is this more fundamental
question which puzzles those who see noble faiths in apparent doctrinal conflict.

It is a long and complex matter to treat this fundamental
problem adequately and fairly. All that can be attempted
here is a sketch of certain important questions and tentative
conclusions. (In passing, we may be melancholy that life
should be so complicated: we perhaps long for a simpler
and more clear-cut religious world: we yearn for the certainties of a simple faith. To these uneasinesses and sadnes-
ses, the following reply is in order: "Sad that life is complicated? Sad that the human race has been so proliferatedly
complex in its insights and cultural creations? Sad that the
sea of learning is never emptied? Sad that God did not
hand us the creeds on a plate? And perhaps you are mistaken in thinking that the certainties of a simple faith are
impossible: Christ asked that we become as children, not
that we become children. We cannot creep back towards
the womb. Faith is not a deliberate ignorance: learning is
not its enemy: subtlety is not hostile to it: perplexity is
not fatal to it. Do you pretend to know God in personal
encounter and at the same time claim to be worried and
frightened by scepticism and complexities?")

A first fundamental observation is this: both the theist
who stresses devotion to a personal God and the contempla-

tive who gains an inner vision appeal to experience. They are not content to say: we are taught thus and thus. They both claim that it is possible to know through experience. Two vital questions emerge out of this fact. The first is that we must take a stance about the validity or otherwise of religious experience. The second is that seemingly we must ask about the relative weight to be attached to the different forms of experience. Let us take this second point first.

We have alluded to "devotional theism" on the one hand and to "contemplative mysticism" on the other. This distinction needs further elaboration and illustration. If we consider the experience of the Buddha, for instance, who attained serenity and insight while wrapped in contemplation beneath the sacred Bodhi-Tree, we notice some great differences to the situation of Isaiah or Muhammad. These latter were in the grip of prophetic experience. This was the dynamic sense of a personal Other confronting them. This was a dynamic sense of a high and holy God who comes in personal encounter. This was not a sort of melting away into an inner light. It was not the eradication of sense-perception and imagery. This was not quiet and introverted. It was disturbing and coming from "without". Here is an extreme illustration of the two types of religious experience. The polarity can be seen too in Christian history: in the divergence between Luther and St John of the Cross, between Calvin and Eckhart, between Knox and Boehme. But it is worth noting that the "cloud of unknowing" in which the contemplative can find himself can be a cloud which is given no divine content. We have already seen that mysticism can be interpreted in a non-theistic way. The Christian mystic connects his experience with the God of Isaiah; the Muslim mystic with the God of Muhammad; but the Buddhist does not make such a connection (save in some of the phases of Greater Vehicle Buddhism).

The two types of experience have typically different settings. The setting of prophetism and devotion is a religion of worship, in which men bow down before and adore a personal God. The setting of contemplative mysticism is the setting of a Path. Very often it is found not in the church or temple but in the monastery or hermitage. The setting is one of yoga: interior training, the mastery of desire and thought. The settings can be combined, as in a Christian monastery. But they need not be.

We have, then, two main types of religious experience. To which should we assign the greater importance? If we stress prophetism and devotion, and exclude contemplation. we shall make no sense of Buddhism. If we stress contemplation and exclude prophetism and devotion, we shall make no sense of Judaism. Such exclusions are theoretically viable only if we have some *special* reason to make them— if for instance we are convinced by psychological evidence that one or other is the result of some deleterious unbalance. But leaving aside such questions, and operating now simply within the context of dialogue between religions, the exclusions look suspect. If both the agnostic Buddhist and the orthodox Muslim appeal to revelatory experience, how can we simply say them nay? How can we simply rule out a dimension of religious history. In short, the drift in the dialogue will inevitably be towards an acceptance of both types.

It is interesting that this drift is not only a matter of the dialogue. It is also a matter of religious history. Early Islam arose in the context of the prophetic strand of experience: contemplative mysticism was not contemplated. But through the Sufi movement contemplative mysticism was incorporated into the fabric of Islam. The converse happened with Buddhism. Early Buddhism concentrated on the contemplative ideal. The worship of God or the gods was at best peripheral and irrelevant. Yet the Greater Vehicle produced its own devotion. It proliferated thoughts of the celestial Buddha who expresses the Absolute in a personal way. The Mahayana thus incorporated devotional religion into itself. Christianity to start with, too, had not much obvious room for contemplative religion: but it was not long in growing within the Church. And so we may go on. The two strands of religious experience have intertwined. They have exercised a certain magnetism upon each other. Thus both in history and in dialogue there is the trend towards the double rather than towards the single.

But if we take the two seriously, is it on the basis of equality between them? Or should we, like the neo-Hindu, subordinate devotion to a higher contemplation of the Absolute? I am inclined to place some weight on the following argument, though no one could claim that it is decisive. It is this. Suppose we take the Hindu line here: suppose we go in for modern Vedantism: then ultimately we will make nonsense of the religion of devotion. The notion of a personal God merely becomes a stage on the way. It is a means of engineering the ultimate enlightenment. The BA ordering becomes fatal to the A. Thus if we are to retain both strands of experience in a meaningful way, theism offers a better prospect. For theism does not make nonsense of the contemplative goal. It does not destroy mysticism. It can hold it in equipoise. The converse, however, does not seem to be true. It is thus no accident, perhaps, that some modern exponents of Hinduism, like the President of India, Dr Radhakrishnan, give a more personalistic interpretation to ultimate Reality than did some earlier teachers.

Nevertheless, it must be admitted that the concept of a non-personal Absolute, beyond the attributes of a personal God, is an excellent counterweight to the anthropomorphism which is so liable to afflict devotional religion. The disease of Absolutism may be indifference to the world; the disease of theism is anthropomorphism. It is a serious disease, for once it penetrates our higher centres we discover a horrid thing: that our word is identified with God's, our prejudices with his, our resentments with his, our wrath with his, our hates with his. If God is a man writ large, then it becomes meaningful to speak as if God condemns the things which we condemn; as though he stoops from heaven to spit at bikinis and nightclubs; as though he helps the British in their righteous wars; as though he carries the white man's burden. All these perils spring from the disease; we can learn something from the Hindu here, for his lower gods may be like men and beasts; but he is clear that the ultimate divine Being is not.

Yet the argument remains. It is one at least which is relevant to the contemporary interplay between religions.

But as we have seen, doctrines are organic. It is not only the doctrine of God that is at issue, but also the doctrine of man. Here much will turn on our attitude to the idea of rebirth or reincarnation. Without this doctrine much of Hinduism and Buddhism would have to be radically re-shaped. For instance, nirvana has classically been conceived not merely as the attainment of serenity and insight but also as liberation of rebirth. The Buddhist saint who has attained nirvana will no more be reborn. What becomes of this doctrine if rebirth is denied? Can the idea simply be treated as a myth? Or after all is it true? Much will turn on the answers. It is not necessary here to spell out all the consequences. The reader can reflect on the arguments for and against the doctrine.

Though the foregoing considerations may, up to a point, favour a Christian and theistic interpretation of the world, there are other ways in which Christian thought and practice are seriously challenged in the new situation of dialogue and interplay. The "particularity" of Christianity is disturbing to those brought up in other faiths. It is perhaps, from the Indian point of view, no great scandal to say that Christ was divine. Indians indeed are deeply respectful of Jesus. But what does seem to be folly and arrogance is the Christian claim that here alone is God's revelation of himself. Here alone is God incarnate—this pinning of God to Jewish history sticks in the throats of the sensitive Easterner.

The reasons for this allergy to the Christian estimate of Christ are part religious, and part cultural. The religious reason is this: that the idea of a manifestation of ultimate

Reality in human form is not uncommon in Indian religions. It is regarded, within certain limits, as a natural thing that God should come down to earth. Thus the Indian tradition is acquainted with a multiplicity of avatars and of Buddhas. It is thus puzzling to make the claim that God uniquely manifests himself in an historical figure. The cultural reason is also important, for it reflects upon the whole social situation of the Christian faith. It is this. If God reveals himself so dramatically and exclusively in the midst of a Chosen People, then the heirs to that revelation themselves become a religious élite. The heirs happen to be (by and large) Europeans and Americans. Thus the religious élite becomes identified with people who acted in a manner suggesting that they were the torchbearers of civilisation. The superiority of the European, his too hasty and contemptuous dismissals of the achievements of other cultures and other faiths, the arrogance of the invader and the destructive energy of the merchant—these vices and threats were seen as entangled in the whole concept of religious exclusiveness. The adoration of the pale Galilean could be a self-worship. The claims for Christ could also be territorial claims. The Cross could become the brown man's burden. Faith could curdle into arrogance; love could turn into patronage; hope could look forward to wearing trousers. No wonder the particularity and exclusiveness of Christianity could seem an extraordinary vice.

The challenge presented to Christianity by all this is twofold. On the one hand, Christianity at the level of religious thinking must endeavour to discover the unknown Christ in Hinduism and Buddhism. A narrow conception of revelation is not good enough, if Christians are to make sense of Indian religious history, with all its achievements, its insights, its sacrifices, its cultural splendours, its vitality. In this sense, Christianity must be "departicularised". We must come to a deeper appreciation of how God has acted at sundry times, in a wider world than the Middle East and Europe.

But also at the social and cultural level, it is worth noting the hostilities engendered by Christianity in that wider world. These hostilities are, no doubt, hostilities to men, and men are often blind and hating. It is no surprise that the trader and conqueror should come in for justified criticism. But this is not the whole story. The institutions of Christianity have themselves been subtly penetrated by certain cultural assumptions. Christianity has too easily identified itself with a certain type of society. It has too easily been an ideology for the European, rather than a Gospel for the whole world. The result of this tendency has been to identify missionary activity with the spread of Europe: it has been to assume tacitly that the Asian or African Christian will become coloured white men. No doubt we here have painted the picture in too sombre colours. Christianity overseas has some remarkable men and accomplishments to its credit. Saints have not been wanting beyond Europe. Christian faith has helped to bring assistance and joy to the oppressed and the diseased. The educational activities of missionaries have been splendid, and have themselves helped to stimulate the cultural renaissance of Asia. Yet it is important that Christianity should be seen with other eyes than those of the European. This is an additional reason why the teaching of other religions (and for that matter the teaching of non-European history) should start strictly from within those cultures—why a sympathetic objectivity is above all necessary. This procedure will not merely acquaint the student with other cultures: it will help him to see his own culture in a new light. This last is clearly impossible if other cultures are simply seen through the spectacles of one's own culture.

Thus the "scandal of particularity" can be the starting-point, not of an arrogant affirmation of Christian doctrine, but rather of a new view of Christianity as seen from outside itself. Such a view will raise critical questions about our own culture. In general, one of the worst troubles afflicting those who think themselves educated is an identification of

the world with their own environment. This is parochial-
ism writ large. It breeds unnecessary despair and facile
optimism—despair because it magnifies our own problems
into the problems of the world; a facile optimism because
it imagines that the solution of problems as they present
themselves to us will thereby mean the solution of the
problems of the rest of mankind. This, of course, is far
from being the case.

Thus the dialogue of religions itself represents an opportunity to see ourselves as others see us. This will be a fruitful introduction to self-criticism, both at the religious and at
the cultural level.

So far we have alluded briefly and inadequately to the
problems of God and of man—religious experience, and
rebirth. From the standpoint of Christianity there is a
further problem—the problem of history. It is an outstand-
ing feature of the Bible that it involves an interpretation of
historical events. It is not merely a collection of documents which express religious experience: it is not just an
attempt to delineate the eternal nature of God: it is not
concerned with ethical injunctions which may apply to all
societies. Rather, it embeds revelation in historical events.
It sees God at work in particular times and places. It re-
cords the self-revelation of God in Christ in a particular
historical milieu. Other religions, too, have their interpretations of their sacred histories: how could it be otherwise?
But Hinduism and Buddhism are more concerned with the
analysis of man's condition: they are more concerned with
timeless doctrines: they are more concerned with a general
prescription on how to attain liberation. There is not the
same emphasis upon the contingencies and directionality
of history. This is not to say that an emphasis on
history is a good thing. So far we are only pointing to a
certain contrast between the Judeo-Christian tradition and
that of India.

The question, however, arises as to whether the stress on
historical events is a justifiable one. Is it right to place so

much importance on the events which have befallen a particular people? Is it reasonable to count historical processes as important?

In one way, Christianity does not have the cosmos on its side. It is odd to treat the cosmos in such a way that historical processes are central. Why should the cosmos conform to the history of men—men who are less than ants on the surface of a diminutive planet in an off-beat galaxy? Can human history reach to the stars? Is this not astrology in reverse—where the influence of men's destinies is upon the stars? Can one man's life, however divine, reach up to the heavens?

Indian religions themselves reinforce these questions. The traditional cosmology of India saw the cosmos as enormous both in time and space. Buddhism imagined a vast number of other worlds. Hinduism saw the universe as pulsating—created and destroyed, expanded and contracted, over an infinite sequence of years. There was no thought here of the uniqueness of man. Even the gulf between men and animals, which was the European background to the shock occasioned by Darwin, was not a feature of Indian thought. Man was a being among others: he lived in a world which was a world among others. The closed, even stuffy, cosmology of the Hebrew world was not present to the Indian imagination. There could be no creation in 4004 B.C., no conception of stars as hedging round the circulating sun. The Indian world was always a big world: a huge world: an infinite world. It was a world (and remains a world) where figures are piled on figures. Vast, unimaginable, numbers inform Indian mythological cosmology. The Bible, taken literally, presented a closed and limited picture.

The sense of vastness in space and time involved, for the Indian imagination, a special valuation of man. Though man was at the head of spiritual advance—though it was man above all that was capable of liberation—yet he was only a small denizen in a huge ocean of life. He was continuous with that life, because he could become it—aspiring upwards to become a mortal god, plunging downwards into a sequence of animal lives. Consequently, there was, and remains, something puzzling in the Christian evaluation of history. The Christian view makes God enter history: it makes God take special and particular account of human vicissitudes. It puts history in the centre of the cosmos. Moreover, it makes a particular direction important, for it finds significance in the Exodus and the emergence of the Church. It looks forward to a final consummation. It does these things without realising how cyclical the world is. This era we live in is but a moment in the time of an eon. This eon is merely the span between the re-creation of the cosmos and its dissolution. How do we know that we are not merely repeating an earlier sequence? Why should we hold our own era in special esteem? Why pick on this eon? Such thoughts arise from the traditional mythological picture of the cosmos which we find in the Indian tradition. They are thoughts which militate against a feeling of significant directionality. They are thoughts which cut at the root of a strong sense of the importance of history. This accentuates the scandal of particularity: it exacerbates the hostility to the arrogant claims made by the Christian on behalf of the uniqueness of Christ. It reinforces the typical Indian view that God's self-manifestation in human and other forms is plural. Where living beings are ignorant and suffer, the divine Being intervenes. Perhaps, too, in another galaxy. Perhaps, sprinkled like raisins in a pudding throughout the cosmos there are avatars of Vishnu. Why confine revelation to this planet? Why confine it to one man? Why confine it to a stretch of history?

These are powerful objections to the Christian view of history. They are objections which are likely to have occurred to us all. They have a special impact in an age when nearly every Western schoolboy reads science fiction and when rockets take off from Cape Kennedy and from deep in Russia. They are thoughts well adapted to the days of lunar exploration and planetary probes. For through these first puny advances into space our imaginations are turned outwards. We are accustomed to think of the stars. We are used to speculating musingly as to whether rational life exists beyond the solar system. Perhaps it is probable that it does. What then of the Chosen People? What then of Christ?

Much of course is speculative: much is mythological in these musings. But still, they raise good questions, and they help to explode our cultural and planetary tribalism. They give us a longer view of ourselves and of human religion.

The Christian can make two kinds of answer. He can say: "History is important because it was in history that God revealed himself"; or he can say: "Because history is in itself significant, it is not irrational to believe in an historical self-revelation of God." From the standpoint of the dialogue of religions and from the standpoint of dialogue with the sceptic, the second is the more illuminating approach. The first approach, however, provided that it is based on insight and not a mechanical adherence to some party line, is not without merit, since God's revelation may underline the significance of history, just as history may have characteristics which fit it for being the context of that revelation. But here let us concentrate on the second approach.

Some clarification, though, is needed. For any revelation, because it occurs to men (otherwise nothing is unveiled *to* anyone) must occur historically. Any religious experience is itself an historical event. It is not then a tautology to say that the Christian revelation is conceived as having occurred in history? Clearly the notion of revelation in history must have a stronger sense than that involved in such a tautology. What is implied is that historical *events* are revelatory, not just that revelation occurs, say in religious experience (for instance, a mystic's inner vision, occurring in 1483). But religious experiences are events, and historical ones. What we want to say is something like this: that events are revelations. It is not just that a revelation to me is an historical event: it is rather that an historical event (occurring to someone else) becomes a revelation. The actions of Jesus, for instance, are revelatory of God. External acts become the medium through which revelation can come to people. The crucifixion, say, is revelatory of God's love. It is in this sense that the Christian claims that revelation occurs in history.

But again what is history? History is, first, to do with men. The process of history, then, is a process of human events and events which impinge upon human beings. Now in studying this process of events (really a whole number of only partially connected processes) we do not just list events at random. We attempt to see how the sequences go, to see the interconnections between earlier and later events. We construct a narrative which makes sense of the developments which occur. In doing this, we are hoping to discern patterns of influence and causation. Finding these is what "makes sense" of the events. Thus the study of history presupposes that, despite the accidents and haphazardnesses which inevitably enter into historical sequences, there are also historical tendencies at work: there are causal interactions between human beings in society; there is a certain "directionality" (not of course to be equated with either inevitability or progress). There is, then, a certain tattered fabric of human events stretching forward from the past.

Why should this be important or significant? One main reason why we would attach importance to the fabric is that its threads consist in human beings. and we regard human beings as important. As far as we can see in our immediate environment, human beings are the most important entities around. Their value transfers itself to the fabric of history: for human beings make up history. But still there is a question. For history stretches forward from the past, as we have seen. In studying history we are studying men in a temporal dimension. We could believe that human beings are important, could we not, without regarding the temporal dimension as important?

The answer to this doubt lies in a consideration of what

it is for the individual to see himself in the temporal dimension. In so far as I may look back on my past with regret or satisfaction, or look forward to the future in hope and despair, I am already treating myself as a "directional" being, and not as a timeless contemporary. Happiness in the more significant sense is a long-term state, not just a present sensation. Our deeper satisfactions seem to commit us to taking temporality seriously. Thus the value of the individual is not just a matter of my value here and now, but the value of my life (thus, for instance, murdering me is to deprive me; but if I were a directionless, totally contemporary being, living for this moment and this moment alone, it should scarcely matter to me that in a second or two I shall no more exist).

Thus the individual already sees himself and others as historical beings. The history of a society is but an extension of the narrative to cover a wider fabric of human lives. Thus the concern for history itself is a reflection of concern for human beings. This is the justification for recognising the importance of history.

This valuation of history connects up too with hope: the hope that present efforts may find fulfilment in the future. This hope might at first seem paradoxical from a Christian point of view. Many folk in the earliest Church looked forward to an imminent Second Coming—a winding up of the present condition of the world. This might at first strike one as a belief in the imminent destruction of human society. But the belief has to be seen in its context. The belief was essentially a belief that the Second Coming would somehow consummate and justify the past. It would transform the inadequate and ineffective efforts of men into a new order. Though the naïve expectation that such a consummation was liable to happen "any time now" came to be abandoned, Christianity retained the doctrine of the "last things". For this symbolised the hope that the directionality of history is meaningful—that the new society in its fulness will ultimately be established.

Such a hope is echoed in "secular" beliefs. The drive to national independence in many an Asian and African country has been sustained by a vision of the new society that will be realised when once colonialism has been removed. For this reason, there is an increasing interest in history in these countries. The Christian view to this extent has become less strange. Again, Marxism, which borrowed some of its zeal and its form from Christianity, looks forward to the ultimate peace and happiness of the classless society, when the State, and the alienation of man from man, will have withered away. Marxism too has its doctrine of the "last things". Present strivings and sacrifices will not have been in vain if they pave the way for universal welfare.

To sum up our argument on history. History can be regarded as significant precisely because it is the fabric of human events: it borrows its importance from the value of men. Men themselves as individuals are directional or historical beings, for a man is not just a present event, but a being who is conscious of having a life—a life stretching both into the past and into the future.

We need not of course be so anthropocentric as to think that human history is the only history in the universe. There may indeed be conscious beings elsewhere. But in our own environment we ourselves prove to be the only beings fully capable of the vision and love which show God-likeness.

If then God is active in nature—continuously creating and sustaining it—it is also not absurd to see him at work in history. It should not be implausible, therefore to hold that God has revealed himself in historical events, and not just in religious experience. But of course the concrete particularity of the historical process will imply that such revelatory events are firmly placed in time and nation. A generalised revelation of God in history would be a contradiction. For historical events themselves, to be historical events, have to be placeable and datable.

This still leaves open the possibility that God has revealed himself in different narratives, that he has participated in the history of other nations than Israel. Certainly the liberal Christian would believe that God has in some measure at least revealed himself in a world-wide way. But the idea of multiple Incarnations, though attractive, has to be tested in a double way. It has to be tested by looking to real examples. For an incarnation is in flesh and blood, not in myth. And those examples must in some way display divine commitment. If God was in Christ he was in Christ: Jesus was not just a bodily form assumed by God to perform a saving conjuring-trick. It is not altogether obvious that Indian avatars would pass these tests.

There is, of course, an easy answer to this from the Hindu side. The tests after all are predicated on a certain idea of Incarnation, namely the Christian idea. But given a different conception (a less radical one), there is no reason why God should not manifest himself in human forms. The argument merely brings out this: that the conception of an avatar of Vishnu is different from the conception of the Incarnation of God in Christ. There is no decisive way of showing that one of these ideas is better than the other.

Yet it is significant that some of the avatars and some of the Buddhas of the Great Vehicle are strictly mythological figures. They do not seriously figure in history. They appeal to the eye of the imagination; but they cannot be discovered concretely in the narrative of the human race. This does not much matter, from the Hindu or Greater Vehicle point of view. It does not much matter because the religious "imagination" is itself illuminating. It brings men insight. It is a preliminary to deeper forms of faith. In the Christian tradition too we are familiar with the edifying stories of saints. It does not always matter too much if these saints really existed. Why always be so factual? Have we not already stressed the poetical and mythological side of the Biblical writings? If Adam was a poetical and mythological representation of the human condition, why not regard the mythological avatars and Buddhas as a poetical rendering of the divine condition?

These are reasonable remarks. But for God to manifest himself in *human* form, it must still be in *historical* form. It must be in dated men, or in a dated man. Human flesh and consciousness are not abstractions: they belong to persons, and persons in time and place. But in what sense can he manifest himself in persons? Does he become those persons? Or does he merely assume disguises?

The latter alternative is a weak one: it erodes the concept of God's self-manifestation. It ultimately turns these persons into myths. (Yet as we have seen, God can speak through myths.) But the other alternative is strong. God is identical with—he fully commits himself to—the incarnate person. But if we say this, then the tests which we laid down earlier apply. We are back with the strong conception of Incarnation; we have implicitly rejected the avatar idea.

This does not settle matters, by any means. But it suggests that the central issue remains the degree to which we are impressed by the claim that God reveals himself in historical events, not just in myth and religious experience. The argument for an historical revelation itself points in the direction of an Incarnation.

These are some of the controversial problems raised by the dialogue of religions. Needless to say, they have here been very superficially and inadequately treated. And we have not indicated an important dimension of the problem: the way in which personal and collective example will carry conviction and insight. Nor have we sufficiently shown the essential flavours of Indian religions. We have not brought out the serenity of Buddhism, its gentle taming of the green jungle of men's emotions, its artistic triumphs, its rock-temples, its splendid poetry, its heavens and heroes, its philosophical subtleties, its inclusiveness, its parables and its moon-lit festivals. We have not brought out the spirit of its great founder. Nor have we brought out the vitality and complexity of Hinduism, with its adorations, its *Gita*, its interplay of opposites, its austerities and exuberances, its river-baths and temples, its gurus and scriptures, its yoga and its faith. All this cannot be done here. But these things must be remembered. They must form the background against which the intellectual arguments flicker and play. They must not be forgotten, for they help to give us insight into the hold of these faiths. They are themselves important testimonies to the vision and love of which mankind is capable. (Of course, there is a darker side: and Christians sometimes harp on it. But this is not the harping of heaven. We remember a text about a mote, do we not?)

Though a Christian perspective on other faiths is not essentially part of the dialogue of religions, as was made clear earlier, but rather is a part of the working out of Christian theology, it is a not unimportant part of that working out. For, from the Christian point of view, it is surely necessary to understand God's activity in other traditions. If we hold, as in my view we are virtually bound to hold, that God has revealed himself in other faiths, then we want to have some insight into the way in which this has occurred.

Does natural theology help here? After all, if natural theology is possible—if men can reason to God's existence —then it would not be surprising if there were knowledge of God outside the Judeo-Christian tradition. Unfortunately, this approach to the problem is not a fruitful one, for a number of reasons. First, if we read the *Bhagavad Gita*, for instance, that splendid and profound Hindu text, we will be impressed by one thing above all. The knowledge of God there displayed is not primarily based on reasoning. It is not primarily a matter of natural theology. Central to the *Gita* is the terrifying, dramatic and beautiful self-mani-festation of God to Arjuna. This expresses a vision easily able to rank with Isaiah's in the Temple. It indicates that the knowledge of God here is imaginative (to say the least) rather than intellectual. It represents an awareness of God in experience, not an indirect working out of God's existence. Second, the natural theology approach is not very fruitful in this connection because one of the world's greatest teachers (perhaps its greatest teacher), the Buddha, left a religion behind him which was agnostic about a personal Creator. Theravada Buddhism today retains this agnosticism. There is no question here of the Buddhist's having worked out that God must exist. If anything he has worked out the opposite. Third, we are in any case concerned with God's revelation in other traditions. This is not a matter of people using their "natural" powers. It is rather a matter of God's "supernatural" activity.

Both the case of the *Gita* and the case of the Buddha give a clue to the solution of the problem. For it is very evident from a study of Indian religion how central a part has been played in it by devotional and contemplative experience. Through different paths, men have found visions —the vision of a personal Lord who manifests himself to the adorer, and the vision of light and peace found in interior mysticism. It is therefore not unreasonable to hold that it is through personal experience, of the one sort or the other, that God reveals himself outside the particular history of the Judeo-Christian tradition. It may often be that this experience is more profound than that of many Christian saints. India has, after all, been a great laboratory of spiritual endeavour. This solution to the problem avoids the difficulties of the natural theology approach.

It avoids them, first, because experience is more than ratiocination. It avoids them, secondly, because we can make a distinction between experience and its interpretation. Naturally the Christian mystic, for instance, sees his own experience in terms of union with the Creator. But as we have seen this interpretation is not universal. If, then, the Buddha took an agnostic view, this is not so much a reflection (from the Christian point of view) on the validity of his experience, as a reflection on the inadequacy of the theism which he encountered in his own milieu. He criticised a certain kind of God. He was troubled too with the problem of evil. It was natural and laudable for him to construct an agnostic interpretation of ultimate reality. Yet he did, of course, consider nirvana to be transcendent: it is a state beyond the perishable events of this world. His was not a modern agnosticism, a scepticism about the transcendent. His was a religious agnosticism. We would only be inclined to deny the validity of his Enlightenment-experience if we were to suppose that revelations necessarily come with creeds written all over them. God remains mysterious, not a text-book. He dwells in the depths, and is not a schoolteacher writ large (however admirable such a phenomenon would be). Thus the thesis that God's revelation is in personal religious experience as well as in historical events offers a solution to the general problem.

These religious experiences are of course interpreted and given meaning by myths and doctrines. The poetical and rational powers of man also enter into the process. The thesis which we have advanced is quite compatible with a recognition of the importance of natural theology. Indeed, there is a vital part played in the reception of revelation by the concept of "another world"—the concept of transcendence. This can be brought by reference to a problem which we mentioned, but postponed. This is a problem which is bound to recur when we think about God's self-revelation through religious experience.

It is the problem of the general validity of such experiences. It will occur to almost anyone in the present age that maybe these "visions" are only the result of psychological and social conditions. Is not the prophet perhaps unbalanced? Is not the contemplative mystic an adept at self-hypnosis? Could not drugs produce such "visions"? These are natural, and important, questions.

They are questions which possess two dimensions—an empirical one and a philosophical one. On the one hand, we can see whether empirical evidence warrants casting doubt on such experiences. For instance, it was sometimes alleged that Muhammad was an epileptic. This allegation has now been shown to be false. Again, Freud, in order to underpin his theory of religion, produced a reconstruction of primeval history in his *Moses and Monotheism*. This reconstruction is mere fancy, without foundation in fact (and contradicted by our evidence). These are matters of empirical evidence. It can so far be said that such empirical evidence has not yet amounted to enough to cast serious doubt on the validity of religious experience (at least in the limited sense that there is no special call to bracket religious visionaries as generally and essentially diseased: quite the contrary). But this is where we move into the philosophical dimension.

For, first of all, what if a visionary or prophet were a bit unbalanced? Would it matter? Some great visionaries in music, the arts and science have been unbalanced. Genius is necessarily abnormal, and statistical abnormality can overlap with insanity. But, it will be replied, we know what great music is, and so can accept the madness of its author. What does it matter, from the musical point of view? The trouble with the religious vision is that we have to accept the authority of the man and if the man is unbalanced, we doubt the vision. We doubt the words about God which express the man's experience.

It is a shrewd objection, but it has two defects. The first is that it is not quite true that we simply accept the visionary's authority. There have been plenty who have been rejected. We think we can detect false prophets. For we have criteria (perhaps not altogether clear ones) which help in this matter of acceptance. First, there are the fruits of the visionary's teaching. Second, there is the accumulated store of religious insight which we, through our tradition, may possess. Third, there is the intrinsic impact of the visionary's personality. The first and second of these tests arise from the fact that the visionary is not just speaking about himself. He will implicitly at least be enunciating moral and religious doctrines. The second defect of the above objection is that the religious imagination itself has proved an important part of human culture. It has sometimes been warped, sometimes revolutionary, sometimes destructive, sometimes creative. Even if we were sceptical about the truth of religion we would need to recognise some of the achievements (moral, artistic, social) of the world's prophets and contemplatives. Even, then, from a non-religious point of view, there would be a parallel with the case of the musician or scientist.

Nevertheless, we are, of course, also concerned with the truth of religion. To cast doubt on the validity of religious experience would be to cast doubt on a whole segment of men's supposed traffic with the transcendent world. It is here that a deeper philosophical objection arises: it is here also that we shall have to recognise the crucial part played here by the concept of the transcendent.

The deeper philosophical objection is that, whatever the empirical evidence may be, religious experiences will be the result of prior causes. There must be psychological and physical antecedents. But if a religious experience is caused in this way, how can we say that it is truly an experience of and from God?

Consider the case of visual perception. If I see a chair, then the chair itself enters into the causes of my experience. Light of a certain wavelength, for instance, bounces off the chair and travels to my retina. No chair, no perception. Thus my perception *of* the chair is in a certain sense *from* the chair. The object of my vision is one of the causes of my vision. But in the case of God, there seems to be a difficulty, for if the above philosophical objection is correct the causes of my "perception" of God will come from prior this-worldly causes. Does this not put the experience of God in the class of pink-rat hallucinations? Here also the causes do not have to do with the content of the experience. Conditions inside me, not in the world outside me, produce my sensations of pink rats. Conditions in the world, not outside the world, likewise (so the objection runs) produce my experience of God.

But matters are more complicated than we thought. For according to the Christian doctrine of Creation, every event is in some way connected with God's activity. God causes the very this-worldly conditions which in turn cause my experience of God. Yet this does not solve our problem about religious experience: for if I see a cat, it will doubtless be God at work. But the content of my experience is not God. Where the content *is* God, surely God must have a more direct and intimate part in the causes of the experience.

In order to make sense of this, two conditions are necessary. First, we must of course already possess a concept of the transcendent—of a realm of reality distinguishable from the flow of this-worldly causes. Unless we are willing to refer some experiences to the transcendent, we shall be confined to a naturalistic account of religious experience. If we start with the assumption that there is no transcendent realm, then of course religious experience becomes empty and worthless, for its whole substance is directed towards the transcendent. The need for this commitment to the idea of the transcendent helps to explain why people can take such radically different views of religious experience: for some, there is the possibility that the latter somehow involves contact with the transcendent; for others, it is necessarily illusory.

The second condition for making sense of an intimate connection between an experience and God is that God's activity should be particular, rather than general. That is to say, his activity should not just be that involved in the continuous activity of sustaining events. There must, so to say, be an intervention. (But we shall later see that this latter term is not altogether the right one.) But how can we tell? How can we know whether God's particular activity is present? A clue can be afforded, though it is a negative one, by our earlier discussion of creative unpredictability. The novelty of the new scientific vision, the novelty of the artistic insight—these we saw as in a sense "undetermined". We argued against a closed determinism which would imply that there is no new thing under the sun. We can apply the same test to religious "discovery". The revolutionary visions of the Prophets, the conversion of St Paul—such events are analogous to scientific and artistic discoveries.

Of course, we could still say that they testify to the marvellous creativity of the human imagination. But if we take the concept of the transcendent seriously, and if we recognise that religious experiences themselves as part of their content contain this sense of the "beyond", then we will be inclined to see such religious creativity as itself being the creativity of the divine Being. Thus once again a crucial part is played by what I called "commitment to the idea of the transcendent". It is notable, too, that this commitment is necessary wherever we count anything as revelatory. Historical events are only historical events, and can never also be revelations, if we exclude from our vision the idea of a transcendent Being who reveals himself through those events.

It is possible, then, to see, in the instances of religious creativity, experiences which stem intimately from the Creator. It is worth adding that once we see revelation from this point of view we shall also be inclined to see creativity and freedom elsewhere (in their "secular" contexts) as due to the grace of God. The doctrine of religious experience that has been enunciated here therefore reinforces our vision of man as a co-worker with the Creator. It also reinforces the view that God's activity is not just a Churchly activity: it is not narrowly confined to the religious life: it is not restricted to cloisters and tabernacles: it is a wider inspiring activity.

But does not this picture still somehow confine God to certain gaps? Does it not channel God's work into the stream of creativity and freedom? Does it not suggest that the human race drags itself along, but gets sudden uplifts through the injection here and there of God's grace? Is this picture not like the one which we earlier condemned—the picture of a supreme mechanic who builds a machine and only intervenes when special tinkering is needed?

This is where we have to examine the misleading connotations of the idea of divine intervention. This term suggests that there is a fixed order which is independent of God's will, which is disturbed from time to time by God's intervening and changing it. This suggestion, however, is misleading, precisely because of the notion of a fixed, independent order. The proper view of creation is the cure for this idea. The proper notion of creation, as has been seen, is of the continuous activity of God in sustaining and making the "fixed" order. God's so-called intervention is not the substitution of divine activity for idleness. It is not an act supervening on a stretch of inactivity. Rather, it is the performance of one kind of act rather than another: it is God's doing A, A, A and then B.

The Christian, more than others, is liable to think in terms of intervention because of his belief in the Incarnation. For this indeed seems to imply that God enters history, as it were from outside. Certainly, the Incarnation cannot be treated quite in the manner suggested by the preceding paragraph. The Incarnation is not a matter just of God's doing A, A, A, then incarnating—as though incarnating is just an activity on God's part, like inspiring people. For the doctrine of Incarnation implies an *identity* between Jesus and God. Jesus is not just a mode of God's activity. He is God, according to Christian doctrine.

Nevertheless, the Incarnation itself need not be treated as an intervention, in the misleading sense. We need not think of God's not being Incarnate before Christ as an absence from the cosmos: for God was present, creatively, everywhere. Admittedly, God was not identical with his creation, and yet in the Incarnation is found to be identical with a person within the created order. But this does not strictly imply a change of identity: rather, in Christ, God manifests his identity.

Thus there is no call to treat God's activity, whether in Christ or elsewhere in history, as an irruption into the order of the cosmos. So-called "intervention" is instead part of the whole pattern of events which represent God's activity, both as Father and as Son. It would be better to substitute some term such as "dynamic" for that which we tend to think of as intervention.

The upshot, then, of the present discussion is this. The philosophical argument about the validity of religious experience cannot be settled except through a decision about the transcendent. Given that we have commitment to this idea, we can then ask whether the dynamic displayed in religious experience can be ascribed to a transcendent source. Two reasons can be offered for doing this: first, the general reason that religious experience itself has as part of its content the idea of the "unseen", the transcendent; second, the theist can link the dynamic of religious experience to the dynamic elsewhere displayed by the Creator. In brief, the question of the validity of religious experience cannot be dissociated from the general question of God's existence and nature.

This may help to shatter the illusion that it is possible to build up belief, or to build up a system of theology, on religious experience alone. As in science, it is necessary to "leap beyond the evidence". It is necessary, if you like, to have a theory in order to make sense of particular experiences. One cannot just begin from religious experiences and prove God's existence: for the concept of God is what provides a context in which we can speak of these experiences as telling us something. Similarly, one cannot prove Christ's divinity from a simple inspection of the historical events. For these events to be revelatory, there must already be belief in the transcendent—the belief in something of which the events are revelatory.

It is now time to revert to the earlier problem which stimulated this rather extended discussion of the general validity of religious experience. That problem was that of a Christian interpretation of the history of other religions. (It will be remembered that the problem is essentially one which occurs within Christian thinking, and is not primarily a question which is naturally discussed in the process of the dialogue of religions.) The solution that was offered earlier was this: that a prime mode of God's revelation in other faiths is through religious experience. This represents a side of God's creative dynamic. Yet does this solution not imply that the work of Christ was essentially superfluous? For if men have access to the divine Being through experience, both prophetic and contemplative, they are already candidates for salvation. What need, then, is there for Christ's saving work?

Unfortunately the Church has exercised its intellect a trifle too much in thrashing over the problem of who is saved and who is not. People are pigeon-holed into heaven and hell. You then meet the problem: Either you can get into heaven only through faith in Christ, or you can get into heaven by other means. If you say the first, then Abraham and the Buddha represent a harrowing pair of problems. If you say the second, you seem to make Christ superfluous.

These problems arise from two sources—from failure to concentrate on the main reason for talking of heaven at all; and from a preoccupation with a certain sort of other-worldly justice. To take the first point. When we think about heaven as being the goal of salvation, it is easy to think that its chief merits as a paradise lie in the fact that humans will have a glorious time. Now in one way this is right; in another way it is not. It is right in so far as communion with God is a matter of joy, not of grimness and fear. It is wrong in so far as it suggests that you can have life in heaven which is sheltered from God. Life in heaven is wrapped up in God. In short, the main point of heaven is God. But then this means that our attitudes about earth should be the same, if we have faith. Communion with God is possible here, and heaven is all around us. The problem of salvation is as much a problem of the here and now as it is a problem of future states. Then we see Christ's work in a different perspective: it is not the work of providing free passes into heaven, but rather the work of God's introduction of himself, and the work of the creation of the new society of which we spoke earlier.

Problems about salvation, considered in the misleading sense of existence in a future state, also spring, as was said above, from preoccupation with a certain sort of otherworldly justice. We think that some men go to heaven: others are punished in hell. It is a matter of reward and punishment. But do we properly understand the nature of punishment? Very often, we think of it as retribution: the point of punishment is to redress some kind of unbalance. The murderer has taken life: let his life then be taken. We fondly recite "An eye for an eye and a tooth for a tooth", out of context.

But both from a merciful point of view, and on the theory of social creativity outlined in an earlier chapter, it is nonsense to inflict punishment for its own sake, as the retributive theory seems to imply. It is nonsense because we thereby increase suffering gratuitously. And it is nonsense because punishment, like blame, ought to have an engineering function. It should protect men and reform men. It should make the world a better place. If, then, retribution is largely irrelevant, a retributive view of the after-life will be foolish. Though "an eye for an eye" may be a useful principle within a general system of punishment (for justice and common sense both require that the scale of punishments should be appropriate to the offences), it is not a principle which justifies the system of punishment itself. Thus a retributive hell reflects an earthly misconception. What good does it do if men are damned for ever? Does this reform them—how could it? Does it deter the citizens of heaven? But they are beyond the need. Does it then just function as a doctrine to deter men on earth? It has been used that way. But the folly of such an idea (and its wickedness) is obvious. Men are to burn for ever, just to keep sheep from being stolen! The retributive hell is one of the bitter prices we pay for crude anthropomorphism—for putting man at the centre, and building God in his image. We distort parables into a system of pigeon-holes. We reduce salvation to the passing of an examination. Shades of the prison-house blur our vision of God.

When these things have been said, it is perhaps unnecessary to point out that the question: "If the Buddha could have a kind of access to God, what need is there of Christ's saving work?" cannot be answered in terms of candidature for heaven. The "necessity" of Christ is not this—that God set up hell, and then found too many people going there, so he had to do something. Such talk misses the poetry and depth of the liberating work of vision and love, and the tragedy of estrangement from God's creative purpose. Surely, we can see that the Buddha participated in the vision and love; surely too we can see that many men, both Christians and non-Christians, have participated in the hell of bitterness and destruction.

But this is all very well (the critic will say), but what of ordinary folk who like kippers and health and bowls and beer? If they are crushed by bombs or splintered by bullets, if they are tormented by disease, if they are cut off young—if, in short, they are victims of this world of ours, is there no redress from the Creator? Are there no bowls and beer awaiting them in the beyond? Surely heaven is not just the joy of being with God: it must incorporate these other satisfactions as well, if there is to be justice. Here we tread on the borders of the problem of suffering and evil. To that problem we shall return later. In the meantime, a thing worth saying is this: "Yes, there must be the hope of redress. But while we cannot see beyond the veil, let us at least note this—that the new society which God guarantees, the new society which we are already striving to build upon earth, is not an other-worldly, attenuated thing. It is a society where we love men's loves, where we try to smite disease, where we nurture the satisfactions and joys of men. The new society does not exclude the beer and bowls. The problems facing us now are what must stimulate us to action and pity. If we have some hope of heavenly redress, we surely already have the call to redress things now. We can employ our love and our vision now. Let us not turn sour because we have to weep for those who are crushed in the world God has made."

The positive approach also implies something about other faiths. We have already attempted to show that God's revelatory dynamic can be found in the experiences which have been so central to other faiths. If the Christian feels that Christ can further illuminate and nurture the insights gained in other faiths, he should not at the same time be negative. There may be distortions and evils in other faiths (as there are in Christianity), but it is more important to see the vision and love which have been manifested. This is where the Christian view ought itself to nudge us towards dialogue. Unfortunately, in the past it has been too easy to go in for contempt and recrimination.

The present chapter has attempted to open up some of the questions arising both within and without the dialogue of religions. It is perhaps well to conclude by repeating what was said near the outset. The impact of other faiths on the Westerner can do much good, by freeing him from a narrow cultural and religious outlook. In this respect, the educational potentialities of Eastern faiths are enormous.

CHAPTER SIX

GOOD AND EVIL

ALREADY the social and practical dimension of Christian belief has been stressed in this book. But there are a number of perplexing questions about conduct and society which have not been touched on. Quite clearly, the approach to the Biblical material from "outside", that is from our ordinary experience, will mean that we shall start in part from our ethical and social concerns.

Once again we may note that certain disadvantages attach to what we earlier styled the "deductivist" view of the Bible. It involves us in the danger of making up our minds before we look at the facts (though facts are not everything in deciding moral and social questions, they are usually or always highly relevant). It also involves us in the danger of anachronism. The moral rules and attitudes of ancient Jewish society may have been useful and important in that context: it does not follow that they can be mechanically applied to the present day. Deductivism has the further subtle danger that we may seek to reinforce our own prejudices by selecting a text from holy writ—thus illicitly smuggling our prejudices into the mind of our God. Thus, for instance, condemnation of masturbation was supported by the text about Onan, though the text about Onan does not happen to be about masturbation.

It is probably more profitable therefore to engage in a dialectic between our current concerns and insights on the one hand and the central revelation disclosed by the Biblical material on the other.

141

A first, and at first sight perhaps rather theoretical, issue which is currently discussed is that of the relation between morality and religion. It has been assumed by many preachers and teachers that morality in some way depends on belief in God. This dependence may be regarded as logical, or psychological, or both.

The theory of logical dependence is the theory that moral rules and obligations would have no force if God did not exist. The reasoning behind this claim can take various forms. It can be argued, for instance, that our duties are only duties because they are commanded by God. This is in line with the picture of God uttering the Commandments. Again, it can be argued that only if moral values are somehow "objective" can they have force: only, that is, if they exist independently of human beings (otherwise, morality, it is argued, degenerates into a conventional system of safeguarding human wishes). But the only conceivable way that they can be "objective" is that they are created by, or form part of the nature of, God. The theory of logical dependence would imply that there is a contradiction between taking morality seriously and disbelieving in God.

The theory of psychological dependence is rather different. It is the theory that (whatever we say about logical dependence) it is in fact psychologically hard or impossible to be good without some belief in God. Naturally, the theory of psychological dependence tends to be combined with that of logical dependence, for if the latter theory were true, rational folk at least would find it hard to be moral if they did not believe in God.

Such theories as are here stated have usually been propounded in the context of theism. It is clear that the dependence of morality on religion would take on a different form if we were thinking of agnostic Buddhism, since here there would be no God to command or create moral values. The theory of logical dependence, indeed, begins to look implausible in the Buddhist context.

Since the theory of psychological dependence is an empirical one, it is as well to look briefly at the evidence. This is contradictory. On the one hand, it is quite obvious that many good and noble men have displayed moral goodness even though they have been atheists or agnostics. It is difficult to argue in practice that disbelief brings inevitable moral corruption. Moreover, the very freedom engendered by scepticism and disbelief can generate liberal attitudes to moral and social problems, contrasting often favourably with the conservatism and timidity of many pious people.

On the other hand, it happens that in Western societies, scepticism is part of, and a part consequence of, social change. In a period of social change, especially when it is accompanied by great wars and brutalities, it is not surprising that there is some erosion of moral standards. Thus there is a correlation between this erosion and religious scepticism. Also, it is possible to diagnose the goodness of sceptics—their concern for humane values—as being a kind of hangover from the Christian age.

Nevertheless, experience of other societies will soon persuade us that there is often a remarkable coincidence between the moral values of different cultures (Buddhist and Christian, for example), which suggests that the psychological dependence of moral ideals upon religion cannot be a dependence on belief in the Judeo-Christian God as such. Thus a main version of the psychological-dependence theory has to be abandoned.

What is more, the logical dependence theory has a number of grave defects. First, the mere fact that God commands something does not make that thing a duty, unless we already hold that God is good. Take an earthly example: if a sergeant-major commands me to do something, it is open to question as to whether what he commands is right. We need, then, the premiss that God is morally good (and thus would not command anything immoral: we need no doubt the extra premiss as well that God is wise, and knows what he is about). But if God is morally good, then he commands moral rules because these are good. He has a respect, as it were, for values. Then the rightness of a commandment derives from its rightness, rather than from the fact that God commands it. To put it crudely: God says it is wrong to steal because it is wrong to steal (not: it is wrong to steal because God says so).

Secondly, the logical dependence theory cannot easily make sense of the argument from the "objectivity" of values. To see this, it is useful to translate talk of values into actual judgments we might make, e.g. "It is wrong to steal" or "It is better to give than to receive". Now what are we saying in saying "It is wrong to steal"? The saying has a close analogy to "It is forbidden to steal". If we saw this written up as a notice, we would take it as an imperative (with an implied warning about the consequences of breaking this imperative). But an imperative does not *describe* anything. I am not depicting a feature of the world when I say "Don't do that". It is thus implausible to look on "It is wrong to steal" as somehow describing a mysterious aspect of reality. It expresses a rule, and a rule is about what ought to be, not about what is. Thus the theory of values existing somehow "objectively" or independently breaks down, because it is not the function of moral rules to describe things which exist.

Of course, things and persons having value exist. My neighbour has value, and exists independently of me. The apple I eat has value, and for the moment exists independently of me (shortly it won't!). A symphony has a certain sort of existence. And so on. But to say that valuable things exist is not to say that values exist (as though they might exist independently of valuable things). Thus the theory of "objective" values is very implausible.

Finally, the logical dependence theory does not account for the fact that it is possible to construct a system of moral values not including reference to God. For instance, classical Utilitarianism, as expressed by John Stuart Mill and others, begins with a premiss about maximising happiness and minimising suffering. One need not believe in God to accept this as a starting point of morality. Yet it may be asked: "Why accept this fundamental premiss? Why be moral, indeed?" Does a higher loyalty help to answer these questions? For suppose that I decide to be moral because I believe this to be the will of God: then I still have a fundamental premiss, namely that one ought to obey the will of God. But why accept *this*? In short, one has to start with a fundamental premiss of one sort or another. Why not start with the Utilitarian one, or with "Love thy neighbour as thyself"?

The notion, then, that morality depends on religion does not have much substance. It is, moreover, a dangerous doctrine, since it is liable to induce irresponsibility in the unreflective sceptic. It suggests the slogan "Don't believe in God, and do what you like".

Nevertheless, it is also obvious that morality has traditionally been given a religious interpretation. It has been viewed within the framework of a whole system of belief. It has been seen as an intrinsic part of the path to nirvana; or as the consequence of loyalty to God. The Bible, for instance, sets morality firmly in a religious context. This is not altogether surprising. For belief in a personal Creator will imply (just because there is a Person there) obligations to him. It will inspire faith and loyalty—and such faith and loyalty generates action. Thus our human-human relations are themselves seen as part of a wider whole: a whole where one has loyalty not just to men, but also to God. A religious morality is not the only possible morality, but it is one with power, because it fuses human relations into a wider vision of the world and of cosmic destiny.

But religious morality has its dangers. It runs the risk of ossification. It runs too the risk of proliferating into meaningless detail. Ritual and moral and social rules become intertwined, so that men can lose a sense of what is vital and what is not. Those who kept the Sabbath to the exclusion of the caring for the sick were suffering from such myopia. Those who are enraged because the vicar uses incense, but indifferent to the sufferings of the poor, are victims too of a peculiarly religious blindness. It is therefore important that we should gain some insight into the principles lying behind moral rules, so that we can distinguish the wheat from the chaff. In the process, we may come to see more clearly the relation between religious practices and ethics.

Let us begin by considering why it is wrong to steal (a rule which commands ready and widespread assent). Two answers are fairly common. One is to say: "Well, if everyone went around stealing the result would be disastrous." The other is to say: "I wouldn't steal from another man because it's not the sort of thing I'd like to happen to me."

The first response lies behind Kant's formulation of the Categorical Imperative as a test of moral policies. According to this we should test these policies or intentions by considering what would happen if everyone acted in the way proposed. Where this would lead to contradiction, you can be sure that the proposed course is immoral. For instance, if everyone stole, then property would no longer be a feasible institution; but if there were no property, there could be no stealing. Universalised stealing would eradicate itself, contradict itself. Kant's argument, though, needs to be taken a step further. After all, contradictions, though deplorable, need not be the worst tragedies in life. We contemplate universalised stealing with distaste not so much because of the ironic contradiction involved as because society would break down.

So what, cries the anarchist? The answer is: so life would be nasty, brutish and short. Without society, men would be overwhelmed with disease, incapable of cricket and cathedrals, shiftless, unhappy. Society is the mother of protection and of civilisation. It is the organisation which has made human vision and love possible.

The anarchist can, of course, reply consistently that he does not care a damn for mankind. Men, he may say, are of no importance at all. As for culture, science and love—they are so much straw. Thus we see that concern about the wreck of society presupposes a value-judgment about human beings. But the anarchist's attitude is in practice not much to worry about. For who can uphold such an austere contempt for *all* his fellows? And who would try to persuade others of the truth of anarchism unless he thought it important to do so?

The prohibition of stealing, then, is a general rule which must be promulgated and accepted by a substantial majority if human disaster is to be avoided. We can cite a number of other rules which are likewise necessary to the existence of society (that we should honour contracts, tell the truth, refrain from murder, etc.). In turn, concern for the viability of society stems from a valuation of human beings.

It is therefore not surprising that we are not only concerned with the viability of society but with the pity and tragedy of particular infringements of these rules. When our neighbour has his wedding-presents stolen, we do not just mutter darkly: "If more of this sort of thing happens, there will be chaos." We feel sadness (or ought to feel sadness) at our neighbour's loss. We feel sympathy. This attitude of sympathy lies behind the second answer given to the question of why it is wrong to steal. We share, as it were, in our neighbour's interests.

This understanding of why it is wrong to steal, both in general and in particular, gives special force to the claim that the ultimate moral principle should be "Love thy neighbour as thyself". For it is concern for our neighbour and his interests that lies behind the socially necessary rules. It is why we recognise them to be good and obligatory.

The Utilitarianism of the last century was thus on to an important point in trying to frame its first principle in terms of the maximisation of happiness and the minimisation of suffering. For this surely expresses concern for our neighbour. By contrast, the rigours of Kant's application of the Categorical Imperative (so that no exception to moral rules could be allowed) suggested a subordination of living people to a moral straitjacket. Unfortunately, however, the Utilitarians did not pay overmuch attention to the analysis of happiness. Clearly, if part of the job of moral rules is to maximise happiness, we need a clear conception of what this is.

Before proceeding, however, to this point, we may note that we find it easier to see what suffering is. We recognise certain important evils which it is our duty to eradicate. The argument that universalised stealing would lead to social chaos has an immediate appeal precisely because we can envisage the miseries such chaos would bring.

Clearly, a full discussion of the concept of happiness would occupy more space than can be afforded here. Therefore, a certain dogmatism may be excused. The first and perhaps most important feature of happiness is that it is sometimes used of a long-term disposition. Thus if I say about someone that his life is happy, I do not just mean that he is feeling happy this morning (indeed he might not be), but that over a long term he is happy. It is true also that "happy" is used in a short-term sense ("I spent a happy afternoon with Jerome", for instance; or "I felt terribly happy when I woke up this morning"). No doubt long-term happiness will contain lots of instances of short-term states.

We may also note that "happy" is sometimes used of a certain context, e.g. "He is happy in his job", "He is happily married". We may call this "contextual" happiness. This likewise is long-term, rather than short-term. Thus to be happily married one has to have been married some time —not because you've got to get used to your spouse, but because you are not a candidate yet for the ascription of a happy marriage when you are walking back from the vestry. It is more natural to ask a man on his first day in a new position "Do you think you'll be happy in this job?" than "Are you happy in this job?"

No doubt "absolute" happiness (as opposed to contextual happiness) normally includes contextual happinesses. It

would be odd to say that a man was happy if he was unhappy in his job and in his marriage (odd, though not impossible: there might be some special vision which sustained him).

A third important point about happiness is that it normally has an "object". If I am happy this morning, it is
reasonable for others to ask me why. Of course, I might just
say that I have an unaccountable feeling of well-being.
More typically, it is because I have just received good news,
or a daughter has been born, or I have gained promotion.
Similarly long-term contentment may in part rest on satisfaction with the way my life has gone, etc. Because happiness may have this reference to achievements, satisfying
events and so on, we can refer to this feature of it as its
"referential" feature.

Similar remarks can be made about unhappiness. It is
dispositional, can be contextual, and is typically referential.
(It is noteworthy that where someone feels depressed for no
special reason, where he "magnifies", as we would say, his
problems, we begin to suspect that all is not well with the
depressed one. Such depression calls often for the doctor.)

The dispositional, contextual and referential aspects of
happiness tell us something about the problem of promoting
happiness, in ourselves and others. It is notorious that an
aiming for happiness is self-stultifying. Those who "pursue"
happiness frequently bring sorrow upon themselves. Why is
this? It is partly because, in so far as happiness is referential, it can only be pursued indirectly. To take a minor example: I may think that I shall be more cheerful after a
day watching cricket. But this is only because I like watching cricket. This is an end which I can pursue. If I gain
happiness (in this case of a short-term nature), well and
good. But what I immediately pursue is the thing which
I consider to be valuable. This helps to explain why those
whose aims are trivial cannot gain real happiness. The
trivial cannot bring solid satisfaction. The Woosters of the
real world are no doubt gay: but this does not make them

happy. Other things being equal, the man who thinks he is doing a worthwhile job will be happier than the one who is doing a trivial or mechanical one.

The contextual side of happiness, which we noted as a typical ingredient of "absolute" happiness, means that satisfaction is not directly within our power. Our being happily married depends on an interaction between two people. Our happiness in our job involves more complex personal reactions.

The dispositional aspect of happiness means that happiness is not a momentary event or state. It thus cannot be gained by a simple plan of action. Very often even a life-policy, which ought to yield happiness, proves ineffective. This is a third main reason why happiness cannot be directly promoted with any assurance. And yet surely the promotion of happiness ought in some way to be an aim.

The solution of the paradox lies in the implications of the referential and contextual sides of happiness. We may not be able directly to promote happiness, but we can promote conditions of work and personal relationship which will nurture satisfaction. We can, for instance, nurture the institution of marriage, which can bring lasting and deep satisfaction to spouses and offspring. And we can promote those ends which men regard as important and valuable. We can similarly attempt to remove those things which cause suffering and dissatisfaction, and those things which obstruct the institutions which nurture personal satisfaction.

The instance of marriage is an important one. For hitherto we were discussing socially necessary rules—rules which, if the fabric of society is not to be torn to shreds, must be generally observed. But a particular form of marriage is not in this class. Societies can exist with polygamy. They can exist with polyandry. They can exist where there is no divorce. They can exist where there is divorce. A whole range of options is theoretically open. Then why do we regard monogamy as specially sacred? Surely the argument must turn on the quality of human relations that it makes possible, and on the equal love which it is capable of nurturing. In short, we argue for monogamy because it is an institution which can in principle promote happiness. It can, we think, promote greater happiness than rival institutions.

The upshot then is this: our general social duty is to help to promote what is important and valuable, and to promote and safeguard institutions which hold the promise of happiness and welfare; conversely, it is to help to minimise those things which make for unhappiness and suffering. But this programme depends on recognising a scale of values.

Here a practical paradox arises. If many people have trivial aims, is it our duty to help them in attaining them? If we love our neighbour, we will love his loves. With children we certainly act thus. Toy guns may be unimportant things; but we give them to children because they are important to *them*. However, the case of children is a special one, in one regard. We do not argue too much with a child over his scale of values, because we recognise that childhood is only a stage of life. That a child thinks toy guns are important does not imply that he will continue to think so as an adult. With adults, things are somewhat different. If an adult spends all his time at bingo, we may complain to him, argue with him, try to convert him to less trivial pursuits. With adults arguments about what is really worth while are more meaningful.

Thus moral and social action involves a double operation. On the one hand it involves helping to promote what people consider important. On the other hand it involves a dialogue about values.

It is at this latter point that the Christian and the agnostic humanist are likely to diverge. The humanist can, for instance, have no place in his scheme of values for the worship and adoration of God. The religious life is not one of his ends. The Christian, by contrast, will not only include worship in his scheme, but will attempt to organise his other values round this one. He will, for instance, see in the deepening of human relations more than friendship and affection: he will see it as a reflection of the love of God. Again, the deprivation of human beings—injustices and oppressions—will not merely be an outrage; it will also be an affront to the Creator who has made all men in his own image. Relationship to God will thus become a focus of referential happiness. In brief, "Love thy neighbour" is seen in the light of "Love God".

The question "Why have a religious morality?" can therefore be answered in a double way. First and foremost, a religious morality is a consequence of religious belief. If we have a vision of the Creator; if we recognise the revelation in Christ: then we shall naturally see morality in relation to this wider understanding of the cosmic process. Lack of religious belief does not destroy morality, but it imparts a different flavour to it: it organises our scheme of values in a somewhat different way.

But secondly the Christian will want to argue not merely that it is possible to see morality in the light of his faith, but that this way of seeing it is illuminating. He will want to argue that Christian belief makes moral sense. He will want to display the insights which can accrue from seeing love of neighbour in terms of the love of God. No doubt it is the task of the individual to work out how this is so. But it is useful here to sketch out two or three instances where this "illumination" is possible.

First, let us consider the kind of attitude which can vitiate moral and social action. Morality is not just a matter of the rules: it is also a matter of the spirit in which we apply them. There is a parallel here with games. Of course the rules are important (indeed, they constitute the game); but playing according to the rules can be vitiated by bad sportsmanship. It can be so vitiated because the rules get applied in a legalistic fashion. The footballer can waste time quite legally, but yet unfairly. Bad sportsmanship also vitiates the game by distorting values: winning becomes all, so that losing generates bad temper, and so that the game

itself no longer becomes an end in itself. (At the inter-
national level, it is no longer good football that is promoted,
very often, but a rivalry in national prestige. This rivalry
in prestige is paradoxical: prestige can only be gained if
football prowess is worth having; the latter is only worth
having if the game itself is worth having; and yet rivalry
in prestige can destroy the game.) At the moral level, then,
there are attitudes which vitiate the applicaion of the rules.
For the Christian, the most serious vice is pride. Does this
emphasis on the evils of pride make moral sense? First, we
must see how the emphasis flows from the Christian's faith
about the world.

The myth of Adam, we saw, hinted that God did not
wish Adam to grasp eternal life of his own accord, through
eating of the tree of life. This symbolises men's fascination
with, and aspiration towards, Godhood. But theism implies
that this is an impossible hope. Man's salvation comes from
God himself, not by his own works and efforts. This is a
main reason why humility is a central ingredient in the
Christian life. Men must be humble before God, and if they
see God's image in other men, then they must be reverential
towards that image. But in a wider way too pride must
wither. If we have been right in seeing the vision and love
of which men are capable as some kind of reflection of the
divine creativity, then we shall see in the achievements of
creatively unpredictable freedom the operation of God's
grace. If I suddenly gain a new insight, it is as though it
comes from "outside". This is not something which I willed,
but something which at best I hoped for. The Christian sees
in his own moments of freedom, and in the freedom which
he borrows from others in his society, the work of the
Creator. In this sense, men and God are truly co-workers
in the creative enterprise.

If we see things in this way the tendency to feel superior
about our accomplishments will surely disappear. Very
often the truly great men have felt humble and astonished
at what they have wrought. The important achievements of

vision and love, in the sciences, the arts, in social revolution, in individual heroism—these important achievements are mysterious to the actors: that mystery is a sign of God's grace; and it is a motive for humility. By contrast, pride is not only out of place: it distorts both the vision and the love. It distorts the vision because reputation becomes more important than truth; and it distorts love, because the other person no longer is treated as an end in himself.

Thus the Christian emphasis on the evils of pride makes moral sense. Pride breeds arrogance and injustice, and these stand in the way of true love of our neighbour. They can lead to a wooden and unfeeling application of moral rules. If I stick to the chief rules, I am all right: it does not matter that I live in an unjust society, provided I am on top. These are the sentiments that arrogance can nurture.

But at another level too pride can poison life. It is not only those who are arrogant who are afflicted by the evils of pride. We all, in one way or another, are concerned with justifying ourselves. We are concerned with status—with admiration from our fellows, or with the hope of good status in the next life. Perhaps the status-seeking is sometimes harmless; but often it is profoundly dangerous to ourselves. For status is something which we have to acquire from outside: it depends on the esteem and institutions of our society. But a desperate desire for that over which we have no total control brings fear and insecurity. This anxiety is multiplied by the fact of death, the inevitable limitation on all our powers, and the mocker of the status which we strive so hard for. It is poor consolation to know that I will have an honorific epitaph. Thus status-seeking is dangerous, because it can breed a sour anxiety, which displays itself in touchiness, irritation and at the worst hatred. Many of the foolish and wicked things which men do can be ascribed to fear. If then pride lies at the bottom of so much anxiety and fear, it is something which poisons life.

The Christian who has faith can overcome pride, not only because of the humility which he feels before God, but by his assurance of communion with God. He will have a vision which makes nonsense of status-seeking. When heaven is all around us, what need is there for decorations? But all this is not to say that rewards and plaudits are absurd. There is no reason why we should not use status to destroy status-seeking—for in a world where status is important, the failure to give status can itself breed the inner pride which we wish to combat. At least we should ensure that people feel that they are wanted. But in the new society the fear of being unwanted will be eradicated.

This, then, is one way in which the Christian emphasis on the evils of pride can illuminate the moral life. Let us now turn to a second, and very different example.

Earlier we referred to the argument for monogamous marriage in terms of its promise of deep and lasting satisfaction. This is so far an argument which is acceptable to the sceptical humanist. Does the additional Christian argument that marriage is a sacrament throw any light on the matter?

It is sometimes said that a sacrament is a "means of grace". This is a phrase which can be misleading. It can suggest that if you want grace, here is a means of getting it —as though by some ritual act men can after all eat of the tree of life: as though there is a magic for ensuring the divine presence. Certainly, however, this is not what the phrase properly means. Rather it is that God is spiritually present to us through the sacraments. The Lord's Supper, for instance, is as it were an extension of the Incarnation. Through it there is a mode of communication between God and men.

But how does all this apply to marriage? Marriage is an odd member of the Church's list of scaraments, for whereas the Eucharist and Baptism were instituted by Christ, marriage existed long before. The Eucharist is a continuing communication to those introduced into the core of the new society by Baptism. But marriage exists everywhere. How is God specially present in a marriage?

The idea that the divine grace is operative in marriage arises from a number of interwoven considerations. First, the intimate love which is possible in marriage is analogous to the conversion whereby we have faith. It is something which comes from "outside" ourselves, like an inspiration. It is not thus absurd to see here an instance of God's dynamic at work. Second, marriage is a remarkable reflection of divinity, for it incorporates both love and creation. The nature of God as Creator is love. In marriage, the bonds of love also are the setting for the emergence of new life. The conception and birth of a child are like the creation of something from nothing. Procreation is an imitation of creation. Third, marriage can or should contain its mystery. Its transports and its successive revelation of deeper layers of affection are a cause for continued and grateful wonder.

Does such a sacramental view of marriage make moral sense? Does it throw light on the nature of sexuality? It seems to. For it presents us with a vision of the creativity which the institution can foster. It emphasises the personal and revelatory character of sexual love—an aspect which can be too easily lost in the solemn and hopeless rituals of the clip-joint, and in the jollier romps amid the hay. It emphasises that the outward physical aspects of sex can be used to express an inner union between persons. In brief, the sacramental view of marriage can liberate people from the illusion that marriage is merely a conventional arrangement. By exhibiting marriage's spiritual possibilities, it is a corrective to a shallow estimate of human satisfactions. To this extent, it makes moral sense. (Yet there is also in marriage a corrective to pride: though love reaches the heights, it is also earthy and jolly, to remind us, as it were, of where we are.)

The sacramental view of marriage ought to have certain corollaries—though these have not always, alas, been perceived by Christians. It is not enough to equate marriage with particular social arrangements, as we have seen. The test of the worth of such arrangements is whether they provide a fitting legal framework for the celebration of the sacrament. It does not follow that, for instance, the possibility of divorce is necessarily deleterious to Christian marriage, for there can be marriages, and social institutions of marriage, which do not harbour the love and mystery which marriage ought to bring. It is a matter for individual political and moral decision. This possibility of choice should not be ruled out in advance by a legalistic interpretation of the meaning of sacrament.

A third instance of the way in which a Christian attitude can make moral sense is the idea of forgiveness. Unfortunately, though the Lord's Prayer has something very pertinent and direct to say about this, Christians have not altogether excelled in the virtue of forgiving others. Also unfortunate is the slight suggestion of one-upmanship contained in the notion that I should forgive others. The Christian stress on forgiveness, however, springs from good theological reasons. It stems from an insight into the loving nature of God, both as Creator and as Christ on the Cross. We are not estranged from God because of his mysterious wrath, but rather are assured that our failures and hates do not present an unbreachable barrier either to God's love or to ourselves. As God breaks down our hostility, so we have the chance to break down that of others. Through forgiveness—through acceptance of and solidarity with those who attack us—we remove from consideration the irrelevance of personal angers.

This makes good moral sense, for a number of reasons. First, it is in line with the social creativity theory of freedom. This sufficiently recognises the important aspect of determinism, that men are not in some absolute way responsible for their acts. It also emphasises that no man is an island: that we participate in one another's acts and affairs. Thus the angry blame of others is beside the point. Second, anger with others is not merely irrelevant, but can be viciously harmful. As we know, it can lead to physical violence. It can lead to psychological violence. It breeds misery and resentment in others. It creates a vicious circle in which by my damaging another person he is stimulated to damage me, which stimulates me to further damage of him. Third, anger and blame miss the vision of the positive aims of our moral and social actions. They obscure the vision and love which we must seek to nurture and engender as a co-operative effort among men.

Thus forgiveness is a vital adjunct to humility in our moral attitudes. We must seek to view others without rancour, and to hate misery and injustice rather than the folk who cause them. We should not be fobbed off by the usual escapes, such as "To forgive him for what he has done does not mean that I shall forget it" (the point is: there is a way of failing to forget that is secretly incompatible with full and true forgiveness).

We have, then, seen that the Christian system of belief is our moral and social situation. This itself means that it is possible to teach the insights of Christian ethics by starting from where we are: by trying to show that certain problems find a solution in the Christian Gospel. This will be a more promising line of approach than a simple-minded imposition of Biblical precepts upon the contemporary world.

This last point is reinforced by our remarks in an earlier Chapter on the nature of our new historical perspective upon the Bible. The sensitive young person, when he first digs deeply into the Old Testament, will find much to offend his moral feelings. The writers ascribed often to Yahweh the hostilities which they themselves felt; and Yahweh seemingly was not above relishing the slaughter of Israel's opponents. It would be no wonder if such a young person were to turn in despair from religion, when it identifies itself with such attitudes. He will have noticed that Christians sometimes latch on to the punitive operations. An unhistorical treatment of the Old Testament is partly responsible for this situation. But the new historical perspective can do something to show the way forward—to see the human developments lying behind the increasing ethical insights displayed in Israel, to see the idea of a God of love, as found both in the Old and New Testaments, as an achievement in insight. The new historical perspective therefore will lead to a *higher* evaluation of the Biblical material than a simple deductivist view can produce.

If we have to incorporate into our ethical reasonings the ideal of promoting human happiness as well as that of removing evils, it soon becomes apparent that no sharp line exists between ethical and social enterprises. There is no essential divide between ethics and politics. For political action also is, or ought to be, concerned with increasing human welfare. Moreover, the ideal of the new society which was started by Christ implies political as well as individual reform. This, however, is where the Christian cause seems to display considerable defects and is open to various criticisms.

First, except in a few countries where Christian Democrat parties exist, there is no political organisation to which Christian loyalty as such can attach. Many would regard this as a good thing, since there are grave dangers in identifying Christianity with a particular party—the danger, for instance, that Christianity becomes identified with sectional interests. But the situation leaves us with the uneasy paradox that the task of the Christian is to work in a Christian way for mutually opposing organisations. Second, too little has been done to work out the particular social aims which flow from Christian belief. So much Christian thinking has been concentrated on the idea that by making individuals into good Christians society can be made Christian that there has been a neglect of the collective enterprises to which men are committed in society. Third, the Church, for various reasons, has often enough found itself politically in league with the establishment. Where this is the establishment of a society which contains radical injustices, as in some South American states, the Church becomes itself an obstacle to the very vision and love which is its task to promote. Fourth, emphasis on humility and forgiveness can be criticised as unrealistic. The Marxist, for instance, is not impressed by attitudes which will soften the struggle. The revolution has to be achieved through struggle and political toughness. The deliberate stimulation of hatred can play its part in bringing about the revolution, and thereby the ushering in of the good society.

Inevitably political action and social reform must start from a given situation. It is thus necessary to see our problems piecemeal. Thus the enlightened person will act differently in the Spanish or Russian situation from the way in which he would act in the French or British. Since one of the great virtues of the Christian Church, for all its defects, is that it comprehends people of virtually all nations, there can be no single Christian programme. Nevertheless, certain characteristic concerns have been displayed by the Church. Typically, the alleviation of sickness and distress have been undertaken by Christian organisations. Typically, too, the Church has been in the forefront of recent movements in South Africa and in the United States to remove racial injustices. Typically, too—though not always from honourable motives—the Church has promoted education. The Church also has done much youth work, seeking to enrich the lives of (generally) the underprivileged. All these emphases are excellent. But more is needed. It is necessary that a continuing critique of the values which men seek to realise through political and social action should be undertaken. Here Christian insights into ethics can spill over on to a wider field.

This represents a real opportunity for the teacher. He can bring out the way in which Christian behaviour is not just a "private" matter, and that Christian values should be seen as relevant to riots in Clacton, advertising, overseas aid, the reform of prisons, and so on. It is also an opportunity precisely because there is no party line to be laid down here. This can give the exercise something of the excitement of a real exploration. The object will be to elicit a vision of the new society, and compare with this a critique of contemporary social values and problems.

The vision of the new society may create hope: but we are bound also to be depressed by the extent of our troubles. Men are rapacious, cruel, stupid; their institutions often are an obstacle to love and to the free working out of individual destinies. Everywhere about us and within us we can see, not the kingdom of God, but estrangement, blindness, hate, pettiness. The depressing facts of man's predicament are obvious, while the vision remains something, it seems, for the future. It is true that we may exaggerate evil. There are joys and heroisms already with us in the world. We should not be blind to the good that men do and the innocent satisfactions which they enjoy. Even so, it is hard that there is so much distress and evil to overcome. No wonder Christians have detected the handiwork and dominion of the Devil!

The struggle for a better and fuller life, both in the individual and in society, seems hard, for the opposing forces seem so strong. Hence it is hard to engage in social action without speculating on the origin of these opposing forces. If Christ has instituted the new society; if God has made himself available to communion with men; if the Creator has made a good world—if all these things are true, how is it that the world as we know it is, for all its splendours, also a dark and cruel place? The call to vision and love itself cannot but stimulate in us doubts and perplexities about the suffering and evil which confront us.

This problem, the traditional problem of evil, is not just theoretical. It is the reason why many good men have, in despair, turned away from faith in God. The suffering of the world was a main reason for the Buddha's agnosticism. To many folk, it seems incredible that the good, omnipotent, omniscient God of theology could have brought the world into existence. It seems incredible that he should allow (and therefore, implicitly, cause) evil and suffering. In Dostoievsky's *The Brothers Karamazov* there is a moving

passage where the sceptical Ivan expresses his rejection of
God because of a single incident—the tortured tossing of a
young baby on Turkish bayonets. This single cruel incident
is enough to indict God. He has produced a world in which
such miseries can occur. A single blemish belies either his
omnipotence or his goodness. Is he powerless to prevent
suffering? Is he not good, that he allows it? This is the
theist's dilemma.

Certain traditional answers do not work. Thus it is no
good invoking the Devil. If Satan messed up the world, this
does not absolve God, who is *ex hypothesi* omnipotent and
thus able to prevent the Devil if he chooses to. It is not
much good invoking the fall of man, since animals (before
men came on to the world) suffered; and because it is unlikely that disasters such as earthquakes have anything to
do with the moral behaviour of Adam or of men in general.
Moreover, if the Fall is responsible, Adam becomes the
Devil, and the work of the Devil, as we have seen, does not
absolve God.

Nor will it do to say that evil is just negative, the absence
of good. It will not do to say this for at least two reasons.
First, the "solution" implies that the world is as a matter
of fact less good than it ought to be. This does not redound
to God's good reputation as a Creator. Secondly, the doc-
trins is unrealistic. Toothache is not just the absence of
good teeth. It is a positive sensation in itself, a nasty one at
that. Men on the rack or being clobbered by secret police
would be interested, no doubt, to hear that their sufferings
are just the absence of something.

Nor will it do to say that evil is like the shading in a
picture. If it were not for the shade we would not see the
light. It will not do to say this, because the universe is not
just an object of aesthetic enjoyment. It is also an arena
where men suffer and are tormented. It is a vale through
which men have to pass. It is also a place where animals
stalk and are stalked, and die of broken legs and fevers.

Nor will it do to try to solve the problem by subtracting

from God's attributes. It will not do, for instance, to say that God is "beyond good and evil"—that his values are so immeasurably above ours that what we treat as bad and evil is not bad and evil as viewed in the eternal light of heaven. It will not do to say this, because it contradicts the assertion that God is love. He cannot truly love men and at the same time be contemptuous of their values. He cannot be a loving Father and count his children's sufferings for nothing.

Nor will it do to say that God is not omnipotent (and omniscient—omniscience is virtually a part of omniscience, for the idea that God can do anything must imply that he knows everything about that anything). It will not do to say this because it contradicts the whole Christian doctrine of Creation. God as creator continually sustains what he brings into being out of nothing. The "out of nothing" signifies that there are no limitations on his creative power. It is not as though God has to work with a given material which imposes restrictions on what he can do.

It might perhaps do to say that the joys of heaven, which are infinite, will outweigh sufferings on earth. In theory, the existence of an after-life solves our problem, provided, of course, that we exclude hell. It is of course an important part of the Christian hope that there is a life beyond. This hope makes the sufferings of disease and torture-chambers bearable. We can perhaps regard the torments of mankind with more equanimity if we are assured that they will be more than made up for in the beyond. But heaven can be too powerful an argument. If God felt that heaven would outweigh everything, he could afford to be careless and unloving in his creation, it would seem. What would it matter that men suffered, if the glories of heaven are so splendid? Of course, we speak here over-anthropomorphically. But still it remains true to say that we cannot bank everything on heaven. In any event, God created the cosmos with a purpose. This was a new order of being to supplement the order of heaven. It would therefore, if God is good, be a good order. The Bible is, for certain, in no doubt of the essential goodness of this cosmos which has flowed, and flows, from God's creative activity.

It is doubtful whether any solution for the problem of evil and suffering can be fully convincing. It is many centuries now that men have ruminated on the problem. We are not much further forward. At best, all we could do is not to find a comprehensive solution, but rather to adduce reasons why faith in the essential goodness of the world is not irrational. At best we can sketch out the beginnings of a solution.

Part of our problem is that we see heaven in the mind's eye. We imagine a better world, and ask why this one which we inhabit does not correspond to our vision. But should we complain that the cosmos is not heaven? It may still be the best possible cosmos. The existence of Mozart should not make us despise Brahms.

The best of all possible worlds? How can we say this? We begin to speak like creators, as though the different possibilities are laid out in front of us: and as though we have to bring one of them into being. This is surely foolish (some would say blasphemous) speculation. Nevertheless, once we begin to say "This world is not as good as it might be" we are already, it seems, stepping into the Creator's place. We are imagining the way *we* would have created the world. The rebellion against God is also the attempt to usurp his place. But this is not altogether a useless piece of vainglorious imagination. It may help to clarify the problem of suffering and evil to ask ourselves in what precise respects one could make a better blueprint of the world.

We could say: "No suffering, no death." But how do we realise this possibility? If men are organisms, which are free-ranging (capable of climbing hills, mastering rivers, sailing the seas, controlling nature, escaping menaces, building cities, visiting friends)—if men then are organisms, it is necessary that there should be the possibility of collision between them and their environment. To range freely is to be in peril of cliffs. To swim is to be in peril of drowning. To eat is to be in peril of choking, if we choose the wrong things. It is apparent that there must be collisions between free-ranging organisms and the more static environment of nature.

But could not God always intervene? Could he not turn water into air when a man is in danger of drowning? Could not nets appear mysteriously below the cliff-top? Could not tar change into wine when we are eating? Could not there always be some divine act which would save us from misery and disaster?

This is an engaging hope. But it suffers from certain objections. First, an organism wrapped in the invisible cotton-wool of divine miracles would not and could not learn. The gifts which make the organism free-ranging would be stultified and destroyed. The hypothesis contradicts the nature of the living, conscious being. Second, the world would collapse into a strange disorder. It would no longer be reliable. While one man is drowning and another is fishing, the water would turn to air, to leave the fish gasping and the fisherman distraught, his boat dropping through the waves of air. The picture is nonsensical. There would in effect be no cosmos if the cotton-wool miracles were consistently in operation. With the collapse of order there would be as serious a collapse of organisms as a hydrogen war could bring. Given that there are to be free-ranging, conscious beings (like ourselves) the miracle-hypothesis is ruled out.

Could not then God at least have set up organisms differently, so that we never did evil? Could he not have stifled the blindness and hate by building us in another way? Could not men have been created wholly good?

But where is this goodness if it is not nurtured by vision? How could there be perfection if there were no insights? And yet insights are bred by learning, by experiment, by mistakes, by probing, by exploration. To be perfectly good, seemingly, we would never have to make mistakes. But unless we can make them we cannot have the insights necessary to genuine goodness. Again we meet a contradiction in our dream of a better world. Consider, too, how in practice we would have to be if we were never to come into moral collision with our neighbours. We would have to be individually supplied with food and necessities, or we might one day in hunger and want have a motive for theft. We would have to be suitably infatuated with one and only one member of the opposite sex, or there would be a chance of rivalry and adultery. We would have to be geared to complete equanimity in the face of danger, or we might perchance have a motive for trampling on our neighbours in some rush to escape danger. And so on. By the time you finished reconstructing men thus they would no longer be recognisably human, and it is equally doubtful whether they could be called good. Their sated self-sufficiency would militate against social life and against creativity. With the bath-water, the baby would disappear.

It seems that dreams of a perfect world *for us* or for beings like us are doomed to contradiction and disappointment. Collisions are part of the cost of consciousness and freedom. Tragedy becomes part of the fabric of a worthwhile life. Our dream of a perfect world turns out to be vapid, or else it turns out to be a dream of a heavenly, non-human paradise. And as for heaven, why should God not, having made it, say: "All this and the cosmos too"?

Thus although we certainly cannot show that this is the best possible world, we can remain sceptical about the possibility of contrastedly perfect ones. This world may after all be the best possible evolutionary world.

To this two further objections will be raised. For one thing (the opponent will say), why should the world be an evolutionary one? For another thing, could this world not be just a bit better? There need not be cancer, for instance. This improvement in itself would mean quite a lot. Admittedly there would still be beri-beri and earthquakes, but things would have improved none the less.

The first objection does not, however, advance us much further. All that can be said is that a dynamic, evolutionary world may not after all be essentially inferior to a static heaven in which nothing is gained and nothing lost—nothing learned, and nothing forgotten, nothing achieved, and nothing failed. It is part of the notion of living, conscious beings that they grow. This growth already gives them an historical dimension. In some form or other, life must be evolutionary, not static.

The second objection is in a way more serious. All that can be said in reply is this: that the regularities of the world may as much underlie cancer as they do earthquakes. Again, the fabric of a regular world brings collision with the living being. This is perhaps a weak answer. It at best raises a small doubt about the sceptic's case. But all that we have here been attempting in the foregoing argument as a whole is to adduce reasons why faith that this is essentially a good world need not be misplaced. Suffering and evil will still present a strong challenge to theism. They will still cause tears and perplexity. If our reasons for belief in God are not strong; if we have no personal experience of God; if we are not sustained by a powerful sense of divine love; then indeed the existence of suffering and evil will wash away belief.

If this approach to the problem of suffering and evil is at all satisfactory, it still leaves us with the problem of how we are to view the Christian's struggle. Against what is this struggle directed? If it is part of the fabric of both physical and conscious life that there should be collisions and hatreds, then are we not in a sense striving against the Creator himself who wove this fabric? Are we not pitted as much against God as against a Devil? God it seems fights on both sides—both for us and against us.

This view is, however, superficial. It misses at least two important points. First of all, it misses the fact that to struggle against a person is to regard him as an adversary. There is no reason at all why the Christian, for all the darkness generated in God's cosmos, should look upon the Creator as an adversary. Such a negative hostility is not only in conflict with the faith aroused in encounter with God; it is also a negative reaction which does not serve the cause of promoting and conserving what is good. It is an attitude that participates in the blindness and hate that we are striving to overcome. Second, the view outlined above misses the point of Christ's life—a life in which God willingly participated in the sufferings and evils of the world, and thus proclaimed his solidarity with the men who are destined to become his co-workers in the evolutionary task of creation.

Moreover, the hatreds and blindnesses of men who have not seen the divine vision and who have not succumbed to the influence of love should, from this perspective, attract our regret rather than our animosity. The necessary implication of living beings in the sufferings and evils of finite existence should reinforce the importance of forgiveness and mercy.

We have sketched out, then, one possible approach to the problem of evil and suffering. It is no solution to that problem, but perhaps it gives us some hope that our faith in the essential goodness of God's work is not irrational. In addition, we must reckon with the "last things"—with the assurance of the ultimate triumph of the Kingdom—of the new society; together with the hope of the fuller joys of heaven. These can further sustain the Christian in the face of the contradictions and perplexities presented by a world which is not fully receptive to the vision and love which can come to men through God's grace.

There is one further aspect of the problem of evil and suffering which well repays attention, though it is often neglected. It is this. We cannot fail to be struck by the mysteriousness, even the deviousness, of God's self-revelation. We may struggle in the world having faith and hope.

But why does God not show himself more plainly? Would not our problems be easier and our burdens lightened if God could reveal himself more spectacularly? Why does he hide himself so obscurely in Palestine? Why should the Bible be surrounded by so many question-marks? Why should divine authority be so uncertain, and Christians so divided?

The problem is well worth attention because it is relevant to our whole approach to the teaching of religion— whether this be construed simply as historical or as doctrinal. The complaint that there is obscurity in God's revelation suggests that there is some better alternative: that God could majestically have trumpeted his messages from the sky. The complaint rests on the need for assurance, for certainty, for security. It also rests on a misapprehension about the nature of revelation and about the nature of God.

The misapprehension is to identify revelation with written or spoken messages, rather than with God's self-introduction to men. If God had blazed his messages across the sky, we would not thereby have become acquainted with him. Our forced obedience could easily have been theoretical and hostile. Faith would be replaced by submission, personal encounter by commentaries. The complaint also fails to take account of the Incarnation, with all that this implies about God's humility and his desire not to overwhelm his creatures. Elicited love is more important than a predetermined orthodoxy. God, in revealing himself, does not subtract from the independence and dignity of his creatures. It is therefore important that Christian teaching itself should not be presented in a way which conflicts with this respect for the hearer. The forcing of propositions down the throats of the half-convinced does not square with the procedure of God in the Bible. It is true that a Prophet like Jeremiah received a call which in a sense overwhelmed him. But this was a call which impinged on his intimate experience. Having encountered God he could not escape his prophetic vocation. But this is very different from the case of the hearer who is willing to listen, but does not yet have a conscious relationship to God. For him to be bludgeoned into propositional orthodoxy does not square with the proper nature of revelation.

It is true also that the Church in its various branches tends to demand the acceptance of credal and dogmatic formulae. But this acceptance is imposed on those who have already come within the Church, and who have experienced its worship, life and sacraments. This again is different from the case mentioned above. Credal orthodoxy by itself does not betray the nature of God's revelation, for it is a framework which constitutes part of the structure and definition of the Church in which the direct encounter with God becomes possible. The Church is a community which continues to proclaim, and to harbour the renewal of, God's self-introduction to mankind. In the encounter with God discoverable in the Church and in religious experience there lies the possibility of faith and assurance, rather than in the blazoning of revelatory messages across the sky.

That religion brings with it doubt and perplexity, both intellectual and moral, is perhaps after all no bad thing. It makes possible the deepening of insight: it reflects the nature of the divine encounter: it safeguards the free creativity of men.

The problem of evil, then, brings us back to the same conclusion as was expressed earlier—that the best approach to the Biblical material is not a deductivist and dogmatic one. The methods and arguments which we have been recommending by contrast involve a dialogue between our own experience and the Biblical material, as seen from the new historical perspective. In this way a synthesis between contemporary knowledge and the essence of Christian belief is possible.

Nevertheless, it must be remembered that this is a dialogue, a two-way process. The attempt, for instance, has been made to see not merely how we can move from the world to revelation, but also how we can employ Christian insights in the illumination of our own world (including the facts of estrangement and the demands of morality). Central to the illumination which starts from the side of revelation is, of course, the work of Christ. We also, however, need a fuller insight into God's total nature. The Trinity doctrine has long been the key-stone of Christian thinking about God. Though it arises out of reflection on the New Testament rather than directly from within it (the idea of the Trinity in its classical form is not directly and explicitly enunciated in the New Testament), the doctrine is one which has been used to illuminate and express both the revelation found in the New Testament and the experience of God in the continuing and developing life of the Church. The doctrine helps to bind up the different strands of thought about God expressed earlier in this book. Also, because it contains philosophical difficulties, it is a focus of honest perplexity for Christians and others alike.

The dialogue, then, between revelation and experience must include an explanation, from the side of revelation, of this central teaching about God. To this topic we now turn.

CHAPTER SEVEN

REVELATION AND CHURCH DOCTRINE

IT is often remarked that the doctrinal decisions of the early Church, which came to be formulated in creeds, were negative in their motive: they were responses to certain current beliefs which in one way or another threatened the integrity of the Christian message. Thus the formulation of the Trinity doctrine at the Council of Nicea in the fourth century should be seen against the background of the Arian controversy. Arius had claimed that the Son was subordinate to the Father—a position summed up in the famous slogan "There was (a time) when he was not" (the Father, but not the Son, was everlasting). Hence the Trinity doctrine was among other things a means of affirming the essential equality of the Son with the Father, and the Spirit was likewise included as a co-equal partner.

This affirmation of the equality of the Son partly reflected the practice of the Church in worshipping Christ. If Christ was not fully God, but was a lower emissary of God, then such worship would be idolatrous. But just as important was the Church's reflection on the work of Christ. If Christ was not truly God then he could not perform the task of redemption, since redemption can come only from God. (At the same time, unless Christ were truly human he could not perform the task, for his death and sufferings would be a sham, and his solidarity with mankind would be broken.) Thus the doctrine of the Trinity is in an important respect a consequence of reflection upon the experience of salvation.

However, the doctrine also attempted to solve the religious and philosophical problems generated by the need to preserve Christian monotheism. The unity of God, as well as his variety, is expressed in the idea of "Three Persons in one Substance". The recognition of Christ and the Spirit as divine should not entail belief in three separate Gods—which would only be a superior form of polytheism. Yet it is easy to suppose that this "Three in One", apparently mathematically offensive, is a contradiction. If a contradiction lies at the heart of Christian teaching, this is surely a serious matter.

Some people are not, however, very sensitive to contradictions in the sphere of religion. "It may be a contradiction," they say, "but it is a contradiction which expresses a mystery." Or else they may claim, like Zen Buddhists, that the heart of religion lies beyond words. Contradictions and paradoxes are admissible as means of symbolising and encouraging the breakdown of human concepts in this area.

Such replies are not impressive. First, it is true that the Trinity is a "mystery". Mysteriousness is intrinsic to the divine nature. But by "mystery" here we do not mean a puzzlement. The Jew or the Muslim will equally subscribe to belief in the mystery of the divine nature, but neither the Jew nor the Muslim makes use of *this* contradiction to express that mystery. The mystery can be brought out by poetry, and is brought out in much fine Christian verse. But it is not brought out by peddling contradictions. Further, once one starts on the slippery slope of allowing contradictions, anything will go. Clarity and consistency in religious belief will go by the board. Intellectual understanding will be eroded. The Christian will look, and be, increasingly dishonest. It is a tragedy if revelation should peter out, as it sometimes does, in fudging and carelessness and intellectual immorality. Finally, the object of the Trinity paradox is not a Zen one. It is not to show that concepts break down at the heart of religion. It is not an engineering tool to bring on a concept-free illumination. It is instead designed to express an important feature of the divine nature. It is designed to give order to our doctrinal concepts.

Difficulty about the Trinity doctrine is increased, perhaps, because it was expressed at Nicea and elsewhere in Greek and Latin terminology which can be misleading to us today. For instance, the term *persona* did not mean "person" in the present-day sense, though it was commonly agreed that God's is in fact personal (in the modern sense). The Greek equivalent, *hypostasis*, means little more than "entity". Again, the term "substance" is misleading, since outside philosophical circles the word is used to refer to chemical materials. "Of what substance is this composed?" we may ask. But the philosophical use, both then and now, means a thing or person—a self-subsistent entity, unlike a quality, for instance, which does not exist by itself but must be the quality *of* something. Thus the original formula meant little more than this, that God is three entities in one being. Since, however, God is agreed to be a personal being, we could equally say that God is three persons in one person.

Do we need to consider that this paradox is also a contradiction? It is useful to consider first the identity of Christ. Jesus, we say, was God. This man who walked and talked in Galilee and also identical with the divine Being. This is, to say the very least, astonishing. But is it astonishing because of the extraordinary fact that God commits himself to human form? Or is it astonishing because of a contradiction?

If we were thinking only of human beings, a contradiction no doubt would be involved in saying that two distinct people were identical. It would be absurd to say "President Johnson is identical with Mr Wilson" (unless we simply meant that President Johnson, being very good at disguises, had for long disguised himself as a leading Labour politician and was known in London as Mr Wilson). Given that Johnson and Wilson are distinct people it is nonsense to say that they are one. Of course, what we mean by a distinct person depends on certain criteria of identity. Central to these is spatio-temporal continuity. A person is a being in a certain place at a certain time, and if he is at a different place at a later time, he can be traced back continuously to his earlier position. This bodily identity means that it is a contradiction to suppose that a person is at two different places at the same time.

Is it not then absurd to claim that Jesus in Galilee was yet identical with a divine being in heaven? It would be absurd, if heaven were indeed "up there". This is why those who have thought in this literal way have seen Jesus' arrival on earth as a kind of travel downwards from heaven. Yet Jesus during his earthly career was surely divine: he did not leave his identity behind him (though it is possible to hold that Jesus was "emptied" of his divine powers). Since, however, heaven is not literally a place—since, that is, God is a transcendent being in the sense explained in an earlier chapter, there is no need to think of Jesus' being identical with a person in a different place. There need be no contradiction in the claim that an earthly being is identical with God, for about God we do not use the criterion of bodily identity.

Nevertheless, a problem still faces us. For as well as bodily identity we make use of the notion of the continuity of memory. My being a single person, despite the great bodily changes which occur to me, involves some kind of continuity in inner experience. If I were a "split personality" leading two separate lives, with two sets of memories which never overlap, it is doubtful whether I should be treated as two persons or as one. The mental and the bodily criteria would collide. But if mental continuity is important, what do we say about Christ? Did he somehow remember heaven? Did he remember his time as God? If he did not, then how was God committed to and involved in Jesus' person?

We can see that the questions are not rightly posed, for they imply heavenly existence was, for Jesus, like a back-

ward continuation of his earthly life. What is more important is the following question: Was Jesus aware of his
divine identity? This awareness need not be pictured in
terms of human memories. Now, of course, the question
cannot be answered save by recourse to our historical evidence. About this there have been disputes. But it is not
unreasonable to see in Jesus' mysterious claims and actions
an expression of this inner awareness of a special relationship to the Father. It is thus not absurd to hold that he did
indeed have an awareness of divine identity. This, of course,
need not have been full and clear throughout his life. It
might or might not have been something which developed,
though there is an implication of the humanity of Christ
that militates against the idea that Jesus was everywhere
fully equipped with divine powers. But at any rate, we can
argue that some sort of awareness of his identity was part
of Jesus' experience.

This awareness need not, as we have seen, depend on
memories. The importance of memories in the awareness
of human self-identity does not mean that there cannot be
some other mode of self-awareness. I know that I am the
same person that went to sleep last night: and to check
this knowledge I can cite the fact that I remember going to
bed and the events preceding. The test of Jesus' knowledge
of his identity with God would be different. But what is
important is the knowledge and awareness.

Thus there is no reason in principle to hold that the
identification of a human being with the divine Being involves a self-contradiction. We are already beginning to
notice that criteria of identity will differ according to the
kinds of things we are dealing with (thus if a rainbow fades
and reappears, is it the same rainbow? Or is it two?). We
may not claim to have a full understanding of the relation
of identity between Jesus and the transcendent being, but
we can have grounds for claiming that this conception is
not self-contradictory.

This still, however, leaves us with the problem of the

"internal dynamics" of the Trinity. Is it conceivable that there should be a single Being comprising three distinct Persons?

The discussion of Jesus' identity is not altogether irrelevant to this problem. For the motive that the Church had in framing the Trinity doctrine was at least in part to safeguard what was revealed. The Trinity doctrine represents the presupposition of a triple mode of revelation—of the Father, through Israel; of the Son, in Jesus; and of the Holy Spirit, at Pentecost and in the life of the Church. One could thus, up to a point, treat the Trinity doctrine in a way which assimilates it to a scientific theory. That is, we can look on the triple mode of revelation as three kinds of phenomena, which are explained in terms of three concepts which are united in a single theory. This is analogous to the situation in physics, where subatomic phenomena, in different contexts, are alternatively viewed as waves and as particles, but nevertheless are brought under a single theory. To this extent, the Trinity doctrine offers no greater a problem than does contemporary physics. To this extent it is inconsistent to rule out Christian doctrine as incoherent, while praising the fruitfulness of science.

Nevertheless, theologians, and this is especially true in the Eastern Church, have also insisted that the Trinity is not just a way of understanding the triple mode of revelation, but represents a real underlying fact about the nature of God which corresponds to the triple mode of revelation. It is not enough to treat the Trinity doctrine as a mode of ordering the phenomena of revelation, though this is certainly part of its function. We are therefore still left with trying to understand this underlying "three Persons in one".

Again an analogy with science may be useful. When radio waves and other such phenomena were discovered, it was thought necessary to postulate the existence of the ether—a subtle medium pervading the world which would stand to radio waves as water does to ocean waves. If there is undulation, something must undulate. But it was found

that this quest was illusory. There is no ether. There is undulation, but nothing undulates. What had misled scientists? It was an understandable adherence to a very strict
analogy between radio waves and ocean waves. In fact there
is an analogy, but it is not as strict as was thought. Science
often makes progress in this manner, by striving outwards
to revolutionary analogies.

This story has a moral in regard to the Trinity doctrine.
Certainly we treat God as personal: this is a datum of
revelation and of personal experience. But it is not necessary to treat the personhood of God in a strictly literal
sense. Indeed, since God is immaterial and non-spatial, he
is already not to be regarded as a person in the way in
which we are. Again, we have more than once stressed the
dangers of being merely anthropomorphic about God. Thus
God as a person has an analogy to ourselves, but yet is
different. This fact is important when we come to try to
interpret the notion of "three persons in one".

Certainly, we find it hard to understand three human
persons in one, because of the physical and mental criteria
of identity which we use (and which were briefly discussed
earlier). It is true that moments and states of great sympathy and solidarity (as in sexual love) can make two
people feel "one". Close social ties can modify individual
identity so that the group activity is as important as that
of the persons composing the group. But these parallels
seem to take us only a small way towards understanding
the Trinity.

The analogy of love is at first sight promising, because
God is Love, and the bonds of human love might therefore
serve to illuminate the inner structure of the divine Being.
A social conception of the Trinity might also seem promising because God's activities must be joint activities of the
three Persons. But the parallels cannot take us far if we
simply retain the literal notion of a person. For then God
becomes three Gods intimately joined in love and perfectly
in harmony in regard to action. This is not enough, since

it does not sufficiently express the essential monotheism of Christian belief.

A tentative answer can be found by combining the parallels with human love and society with a modified concept of the person. Of course, we cannot know what it would "feel like" to be God. In this sense there is a grave limit on our having a good understanding of divine personhood. But we can sketch out tentative analogies which may serve to break down the concept of a person as we understand it, to make room for a different concept which can be applied to God.

For instance, we already possess a type of experience which can point to a conception of two "lives" led by one person. In dreaming, I lead a life which is up to a point autonomous in relation to the waking life. Yet in waking, I can be aware of my dream life. The "autonomy" of my dream life means that I take decisions in my dreams which I do not necessarily approve of in my waking (a point which has been shown, in the Freudian era, to be of profound psychological significance, for the dream decisions often represent real desires which I scarcely acknowledge to myself when waking). This disharmony between dreaming and waking demonstrates a limitation upon the full integration between my actions and my desires; but it also exhibits, albeit dimly, the possibility of two lives shared by a single consciousness. If we extend this possibility, by breaking beyond the bounds of our own experience (and we have to do this to have any sort of theoretical understanding of God's nature), then it is possible to conceive of two lives led by the same person. Where, *ex hypothesi*, personhood is not defined by bodily identity, the two lives can themselves be said to constitute persons. We can thus construct an idea of two or three persons who yet share the same underlying identity. It becomes possible to think of "three Persons in one".

The parallels with love and with society then come into their own. The harmony of the lives and their interlocking sympathy represent a parallel to human love, though in human love there are necessary limitations, so that, glorious as it is, it can only point rather dimly towards the full glory of the inner divine love. The "group" activity of the three divine lives is social, but free from the conflicts which we experience in human society, since there is interlocking responsibility for and approval of the actions performed in the three divine lives.

If this picture of the Trinity is at all accurate, it in turn may serve to illuminate human life. It is true that here we have tried to work upwards from human experience to the nature of God. But the problem presents itself only because already God has revealed himself in a triple mode of activity. Essentially we are not doing natural theology here. Essentially we are trying to explicate revelation. Thus we are still moving from the side of revelation, in the dialectic between revelation and experience. We therefore wish to know how far the Trinity doctrine itself can throw light upon the human predicament (beyond the light already thrown upon it by the work of the Creator and the work of Christ in redemption—aspects of revelation which have already been discussed). The answer to this question is twofold. First, and most relevantly to the preceding discussion, there is the way in which the internal dynamic of the Persons of the Trinity can say something about human life. Second, there is the role of the Spirit, which hitherto has been left on one side. Indeed, the doctrine of the Spirit tends to be much neglected in expositions of Christian belief these days.

On the first issue: the internal dynamic of the Trinity can say something to us about the nature of the new society, the Kingdom. The interpenetrating love, and the harmony in creative action, of the Trinity can be an ideal (not fully realisable, because of the special nature of the divine "three in one" society), through which we can pattern our own strivings. The internal dynamic of the Trinity, as an ideal, can help to reinforce the need for "participating" in each

other's acts, which we saw as a consequence of the social
creativity theory of freedom. The aim of the Christian,
through this participation, is to reduce the disharmony
between men. Here something can be learned from Marxism, which has put the discussion of disharmony or alienation on a new basis, by calling attention to the material
and economic factors which lead to class (and other) conflicts. The Marxist solution, of exacerbating present class
conflict as a preliminary to the revolution which will ultimately issue in a classless and thus harmonious society, can
well be criticised, partly because there are in some societies
alternative methods of social revolution, partly because the
wrong kind of hatred is induced, partly because alienation
does not disappear so easily as was hoped, partly because
the economic assumptions of Marxism are too crude.
Nevertheless, Marxism has generated in men the hope of
ultimate social harmony, and this hope conforms to the
pattern of Christian expectation. Marxism, too, by empha-
sising so strongly the material and economic factors in the
alienation of men from their environment, can restore to
Christianity a vision of Christian "materialism". The internal dynamic of the Trinity includes the whole experience
of Incarnation. This Incarnation points us unmistakably
to the ideal of transforming the material and social world.

The pattern of the Trinity can therefore determine for us
some tests for our social and political activity. First, does
acquiescence in a particular social or political situation
make for ultimate harmony or disharmony? For instance,
the struggle for national independence in a colonial country
expresses a rejection of a particular socio-political structure: normally, it can be argued that the struggle makes
for harmony in the long run, because of the manifest divi-
sions and injustices, both political, personal and economic,
consequent upon colonial status. Second, does a particular
means of social change make for harmony or disharmony?
There is not necessarily a choice of means: if a country is
already in civil war, the means of peaceful non-violence is

ruled out. But where there is a choice, as in the South of the United States, the Christian answer has been plain. Third, does the maintenance, in a given society, of a Christian resistance to the prevailing structure make for or against creativity and love? The structure of the Trinity is dynamic, as well as harmonious. It expresses what we would call a "full life". The Christian in society must therefore see in the preservation of a Christian community not just a means of preserving a tradition, nor just a means of preaching the Gospel (vital as this may be); but also he must see it as a means of protest against forces which induce conformism, which is the enemy of the dynamic development of personality and of cultural creativity. (Unfortunately, the Church has not always had a good record in this respect.) Mass culture from "below" and ideology from "above" are alike liable to erode persons. Fourth, in a given struggle, does the Christian genuinely identify himself with his "enemies"? It is ultimately only by transforming the situation of those who are led to stupidities and violence that real harmony will be obtained. It is not sufficient to struggle against blindness and hate; it is necessary to bring them to see a nobler vision. In this way, we can participate in their predicament.

These then are some of the tests of social action which arise out of reflection upon the harmonious inner dynamic of the Trinity. At the personal level, also, the Trinity doctrine may help us, for that inner harmony or wholeness which is the peace of God cannot be realised by a sort of inner conformism. The fault of much virtue has been that it has been bought at a great expense, in stifling emotions which then find their outlet in punitive attitudes towards those who do not exhibit such virtue, and in inner mental turmoil. Here the ideal of the Trinity shows the need of harmony between our different "lives". Traditionally, Christianity has stressed the need for faith in this process towards wholeness. This is only another way of saying that conversion must involve a changing round (a conversion) of motives, rather than the imposition upon ourselves of a complex of rules in which we do not have our hearts. All this is reinforced by modern discoveries in psychology, and by modern practices in psychological medicine.

Marx, Gandhi and Freud in different, and admittedly incomplete and sometimes mistaken ways, contribute to our understanding of the way forward in social and personal change. It is no coincidence that the doctrine of the Trinity —the notion of Incarnational dynamism in a setting of inner and outer harmony—helps to illuminate and to bring together the new insights that these and other men have reached. It is a ground of Christian optimism that these "new prophets" should have helped to restore and to enlarge the Christian conception of the new society.

So much, briefly and inadequately, for the first phase of the answer to the way in which the Trinity is relevant to our contemporary concerns. We now turn to the specific problem of the Spirit.

The Spirit, as is stressed in the Bible, is the Spirit of truth. But what, as Pilate asked, is truth? In the Christian tradition, the work of the Spirit has been seen as being oriented primarily towards the illumination of the Truth expressed in Christ. The Spirit, coming in power at Pentecost, produced a revolution in the vision of the earliest Church. Through the light shed by the Spirit men were able to see the full nature of Jesus, and through this vision to go forward and outward in the work of bringing the divine revelation to men. Gradually, through the work of the Spirit, the Church was enabled to frame a fuller and deeper picture of the whole divine action and purpose. But the vision of the Truth was always accompanied by an access of power. This is why the Holy Spirit is so intimately associated with the solemn moments in the Church's life, in which this power is communicated and handed on. But herein there lies a danger, or a set of dangers.

There is the danger that the Christian will see the Holy Spirit as *confined* in his activity to the Church's life, as though the Spirit is simply on tap to justify and sustain ecclesiastical practices. There is the danger that a narrow idea of "power" will prevail. Thus, though it is true that the Apostles, under the influence of Pentecost, spoke with tongues (so that some among the audience thought them drunk), it is too easy to identify the Spirit with such "outpourings", when they were but symptomatic of the strange new dynamism of the Church. There is, too, the danger that the life of the Spirit is thought of as being confined in time, as though the Spirit did not exist before Pentecost. These dangers in different ways reflect the reluctance to think of the Spirit as in a full sense divine, but rather as an offshoot of the activity of God.

The dangers in question can be combated by a fuller appreciation of the real meaning of the Spirit as giver of truth and power. Although, for the Christian, Christ is the Truth, it does not follow that the truth is restricted to theological or other propositions about Christ. Although the power of divine love is primarily channelled through the Church, it does not follow that propositions about divine love are restricted to talk about the Church or its sacraments. Heaven forbid. Here we are faced with a principle which has run through so much of the discussion in this book—that Christian belief is not just about "revelation" as narrowly considered. It is about the whole world, the whole cosmos. Revelation is the central point in the illumination of the cosmos. But the cosmos as a whole is the theatre and expression of God's creative activity. We must repudiate a small, finite God who spends his efforts covenanting with the old and new Israel. For God is Creator of the world, and cannot thus be restricted and confined. Just as I may reveal myself in my expressions, and yet also be operative in my walking and eating and thinking, so God, though he reveals himself par excellence in the history of Israel and of the Church, also is operative in countless ways throughout the vast universe which he has created and which he continually sustains. Consequently, we must see the activity of the Spirit in a broader way than that indicated by the three "dangers" which we listed in the preceding paragraph.

A clue to this wider perspective is found when we consider the role of the Spirit as the One who creates the response of faith, involving both a vision of the truth and the access of divinely inspired power. We have elsewhere attempted to argue, in this book, that creative vision and love, wherever they occur, can be attributed reasonably, from the Christian point of view, to the grace of God. We can deepen this claim, by seeing creative vision and love as essentially the work of the Spirit. Here is a wider way in which God is operative in history.

But this thesis itself needs further clarification. For at first sight it looks as though the Spirit is just another form of Incarnation. The Spirit, we might think, is God active in human genius and heroism. This is too restricted a view, still, and for a number of reasons.

First, we must remember the setting of the vision and love which reflect the creative activity of God. The setting is that of an interaction between human beings and their material and social environment. For instance, the visual arts represent of complex interplay between the world as accessible to human perception and the imagination displayed by the artist. The understanding of the physical world depends upon, in part, our capacity to observe and manipulate things around us. The truths of science are truths, then, about our milieu. It is thus false to look upon what we have in this book called "vision" as though it springs silently from within human consciousness. To put the matter crudely: vision has an object as well as a subject. By consequence, the arising of vision represents a transaction between man and nature. In Christian terms, it is a transaction between God's grace within and God's nature without. Here the doctrine of the Spirit may find a special relevance and a special interpretation. To speak of grace "within" and nature "without" is to point to the dialectic between vision and its object. But strictly the creative act is a consequence of this dialectic. It does not come simply from within or from without. If, then, the creative vision is a (so to say) joint product, then we can see the work of the Spirit, as being active in the production of the creative vision, as being jointly from within and from without. It expresses a link between nature, which is itself the expression of God's creative powers, and humanity. This "linking" reflects the activity of the Spirit in bringing men to the Truth in Christ, for here too faith comes both from "within" and from "without", both from the heart of men and from the revelation in Christ. Thus the Spirit has a special place in linking God's general creativity to the creativity of human beings. He is not to be considered as an incarnation within humans, but as the creative factor wherever there is a dialectic between conscious beings and the natural order.

Again, as this last remark suggests, the work of the Spirit need not be restricted to a relationship between God and human beings. Elsewhere in the cosmos, it may be, there is a similar dialectic at work, though we may never know of this. Further, it must be stressed that the Spirit remains a transcendent Being, as do the other Persons of the Trinity. His life is not confined to the power and truth which he may generate on earth or elsewhere, for his life is part of the inner dynamic of the divine nature.

It may be remarked in passing that the idea that God is "deep down" rather than "out there"—an idea expressed rather forcibly in *Honest to God*—is relevant to thought about the Spirit. It is true, as we said in an earlier chapter, that "deep down" can no more be taken literally than "out there", and it is a pity that the Bishop of Woolwich did not spend more time in trying to analyse the notion of transcendence. Nevertheless, the picture presented by the talk of "deep down" points us towards an appreciation of God's activity within, as we say, the "depths" of human personality. The picture is a fairly suitable one for trying to express the work of the Spirit, both in creating vision and in creating love. This is perhaps the chief merit of the book, that it sketches a possible way of revitalising belief in the Spirit —even if the "deep down" analogy does not bring out sufficiently the way in which vision results from the dialectic with nature, and love from an analogous reciprocity between person and person in community.

The doctrine of the Spirit, then, is one which has to do with much more than the Church and with religion, as narrowly conceived. This means that the Church's faith in the Spirit can help to illuminate the tasks facing men. It can do so because it shows both the origin and destination of men's creative powers. The origin lies in the vision and power through which men have become co-workers with God, whether this co-working be recognised or not. The destination is revealed through the linking activity of the Spirit. For the Spirit not only links men and nature in the creative dialectic by which new truth is discovered and new possibilities of human love are realised, but he also links this truth and love with the Truth in Christ. The Spirit points outwards into nature, but also inwards to Christ. This implies that the ultimate harmony is to be discovered in a society which is at one with Christ. In brief, the new society instituted by Christ must embrace the insights and achievements of mankind as a whole.

This in turn tells us something about the whole problem of the relation between revelation and "secular" knowledge and experience. It has been a main theme in this book that Christianity must not only be understood, but must also be taught, in the context of a dialectic between our own experience and revelation. At certain points, we approach revelation from the side of our immediate experience. At others we approach our experience from the side of revelation. This dialogue between tradition and modern knowledge is only part of the "linking" process associated with the work of the Spirit. Thus the doctrine of the Spirit itself reinforces the need for, and explains the fruitfulness of, the Christian dialogue with the so-called secular world.

This notion of a dialectic is important educationally, because it brings out the way in which understanding is not a one-way process. It was a merit of Socrates' idea that teaching was like midwifery that he recognised the need to elicit understanding from within the other person. This, at least, is one half of the dialectic of learning. Similarly, religious education has to involve a dialectic between the experience of the hearer and the nature of revelation. The foregoing arguments in this book have been an attempt to exhibit, at a philosophical and theological level (though doubtless not a profound one) the kind of dialogue which is possible between our current knowledge of the world and the central aspects of Christian revelation.

But it may be justly complained that this approach to Christian belief has in one way been too "theoretical". Or at least that it has been too philosophical and theological. Even if the results of the arguments contained in the book were accepted (and I only present them as possibilities, not as a framework for some party line)—even were these results accepted, there still remains a large gap between the arguments used here and the teaching of religion in schools and elsewhere.

To this problem of the supposed gap, I shall turn in the next chapter. Meanwhile, one corollary of the preceding discussion of the Trinity and the Spirit is worth bringing out. Though we have been at pains to show the relevance of revelation to the wider world and to society, it remains true that this revelation, as mediated through the Bible and through the doctrines of the Church, has found its primary response among those who have constituted the Christian community. That is, revelation has primarily occurred within the Church. Thus faith has been a response in a certain setting: in the setting of worship, prayer, the sacraments and so on. This "religious" setting means that Christian doctrine is neither simply metaphysical nor simply

ethical and social: it is also profoundly involved with the
whole process of worship. Hence the dialectic between
revelation and "secular" experience must also be seen as a
dialectic between worship and other activities. It is worth
bringing out this corollary, precisely because the teaching
of the Bible, or of doctrine, or of Christian ethics, tends to
occur in a setting divorced from the worshipping activity
of the Church. This is another gap between theory and
practice; but it can partly be filled by the very recognition
that it exists, and partly by a proper appreciation of the
poetical elements in the scriptural tradition, which themselves are often hymns, and therefore means of expressing
worship.

CHAPTER EIGHT

IS THEOLOGY RELEVANT?

IT might be thought, as was remarked near the end of the preceding chapter, that a philosophical and theological discussion of transcendence, science, the human predicament and the Trinity is not directly relevant to the teaching of religion (except to those who wish to be theologians or philosophers). Is there not a gap between such theology and the actual task that the teacher has in hand?

There is a gap: but it has been the assumption throughout this book that the gap is to be bridged by the teacher. There can be no special version of theology which replaces the interplay between the teacher and his pupils. This interplay presupposes that the teacher has at least some tentative outline of the way in which he views the different aspects of religion. It is at this level that there is the need for an acquaintance with the main philosophical and theological issues. But again this "acquaintance" need not (indeed should not) be a simple reception of a system of propositions. Both philosophy and theology require instead, in differing ways, a real engagement of the individual with the problems. Both should be disturbing as well as exciting. Consequently, the philosophical and theological arguments presented in this book are intended merely as a stimulus through which the teacher can clarify his own ideas through an engagement with the chief questions. If anyone feels that he has good reason to reject the whole or part of what has been argued here, I for one shall be quite content, for such a reasoned rejection will imply engagement with the problems which I think are important in this area.

It is, then, only after the clarification that the teacher is in a position to plot the strategy and tactics of his teaching. Naturally, this is an oversimplification, since the teaching itself will produce further shifts and clarifications. Nevertheless, it is almost hopeless to approach the teaching of the Biblical material without having some general *point of view*. The aim of this book has been to present one possible point of view, even if only as a cockshy.

Thus the answer to the objection about the gap is this. The person who must fill the gap can only do so if that gap is a gap between a point of view and the procedures of teaching. If there is no point of view, admittedly the gap becomes infinite, and the consequence is that the real process of teaching can never be reached. The point of view necessarily involves some kind of theological reflection (even for the atheist). Theology is therefore relevant to the process of teaching, but in an indirect way.

However, in another way theology may throw light on the pattern of religious education. Though there is no question here of trying to replace the skills and insights of the teacher by laying down any fixed scheme either of belief or of syllabus, it may nevertheless be possible to explore some tentative guiding principles. These principles themselves flow from the type of approach to theological and philosophical problems already adopted in this book.

It is intrinsic to this approach that we should participate in a dialectic between revelation and contemporary knowledge. Now admittedly many of the important issues in such a dialectic may lie beyond the intellectual horizon of some of those who are being taught (though not as far as one might at first think, for many of the "simpler" puzzlements about religion expressed by children from the time when they become critical of what they have hitherto learned about religion—say from the mental age of 12— are puzzlements which essentially go deep into philosophical and theological problems). But even though the full dialectic between revelation and modern knowledge cannot be exhibited until people have reached intellectual maturity, the principle of the dialectic can be used in teaching. This means a two-fold process.

On the one hand, it means that the teaching can move from contemporary phenomena to revelation. On the other hand, it means that we can move from revelation to contemporary phenomena. The ways in which this can be done can be illustrated by two examples, at a relatively simple level. Many children will have read about, or seen on television, or, worse, experienced at first hand, the prejudices and violences generated in our cities, and in the U.S. and elsewhere, by racial distinctions. Enmities between different groups, of course, are no new thing. The same kind of enmity existed between the Jews and the Samaritans. The latter were regarded both socially and religiously as outcastes. Here then is a Biblical analogue to contemporary enmities, and in this light it is possible to make living sense of various passages in the New Testament, notably the Parable of the Good Samaritan and Jesus' conversation with the Samaritan woman at the well. Conversely, one can begin with one or other of the stories of Jesus' healing miracles, and elucidate their significance today. Is it just that Jesus was showing off strange powers? Or was there a deep compassion which can illustrate to us the relation between the work of God and the whole present-day apparatus of succour, such as the Red Cross and the hospitals?

But the dialectic between "now" and "then" will remain ineffective unless two further principles are applied. What I may call the "dialectical" principle must be supplemented by the principles of historical realism and of progressive understanding. These are as follows.

The principle of historical realism flows from the adoption of what I have called earlier the "new historical perspective". The fruits of modern scholarship have been profound in uncovering the historical setting and meaning of many incidents in the Bible which would otherwise be relatively unclear to us. From archaeological and other evidence we now have a fairly good grasp of what life was like at different points in the history of Israel down to the time of Jesus. This new knowledge gives us an immense opportunity to make the Biblical material more concrete, more living. It is an opportunity to give the narratives the same kind of life which other histories have, instead of treating the Biblical world as static and half unreal. We are, for instance, able more clearly to enunciate the political and religious choices which lay before Jesus, and the political and religious expectations held by different groups among those who at one time or another supported him. The bringing out of what life was like, and what the choices were, requires imagination and knowledge. But it has the promise of giving historical realism to the narratives which we have.

It is true that this historical realism will have as a side-effect the uncovering of some doubtful emphases in the narrative, and even errors and suppressions. For instance, the Gospel accounts of Jesus' trial and death lay the blame for his execution primarily on the Jews as a collective body, speaking both through their "establishment" (the Sanhedrin) and through the mob which cried out "Crucify him". It is doubtful, to say the least, that the blame can be so simply and indiscriminately assigned (and Jesus himself said "Father, forgive them", in any case). It is therefore a necessary corollary of the principle of historical realism that students of religious knowledge shall become increasingly and more sensitively aware of the milieu in which the Biblical material was put together, and the nature of this process of writing and editing. Thus the principle of historical realism will ultimately mean that what we earlier called "deductivism" will be eroded. Some might think that the effect of this will be deleterious. Will it not shake children's faith in the authority of the Bible? This I doubt, and for two reasons.

First, authority is not a matter of "speaking down". It must flow from real respect, not from inviolable eminence. The life of Jesus is a case in point. He spoke as one with authority, but he did not come with an army of angels: quite the reverse. Similarly, a sense of Jesus' authority, despite the defects which may exist in the written accounts of his teaching and work, comes unmistakably through to us. Nor is this all. The accumulation of archaeological and historical evidence gives us reason to treat the Biblical material, if not slavishly, yet with respect as a source of historical knowledge. Ultimately, then, the principle of historical realism will enhance, rather than diminish, a real feeling of respect for the material. Secondly, an uncritical treatment of the Bible lands us with swallowing the whale that swallowed Jonah, and with accepting quite a number of strange stories as literal fact. Of course, we ought to be discriminating (truth is sometimes stranger than fiction). Nevertheless, uncritical attitudes to the Bible will inevitably confer on it the status of a fairy tale. Children know from their own experience that adults like to tell them tales, such as those about Santa Claus. When you grow up, you see through them, though you don't necessarily blame your parents (such tales once gave you pleasure). A similar attitude to the Bible will arise from an uncritical presentation. It is no accident that hitherto the teaching of religious knowledge in schools, often by those who, usually through no fault of their own, are not equipped to employ the principle of historical realism, should have seemingly induced more atheism than religious sensitivity. Consequently, we can regard it as a blessing that the principle of historical realism has as its corollary a critical awareness of the ways in which the Biblical material was put together.

Clearly, of course, there are limits to the extent of this critical awareness. An expert and detailed grasp of the processes of composition of the Biblical material is the product, necessarily, of considerable specialisation. But it is surely important that a general grasp of the processes should be induced, in the course of the attempt to stimulate the historical imagination.

There is an aspect of the principle of historical realism which, because of the nature of the Bible, deserves separate mention. The Bible is, obviously enough, a mainly religious book. It therefore incorporates a whole set of religious ideas, spanning many centuries of development. It is not always easy for those who live in a society such as that of Britain to understand fully the impact of these ideas. The ancient Jews employed different kinds of animal sacrifice, for example. Few of us have had the opportunity to visit a country where animal sacrifice is still performed. To know what it is like and to appreciate the significances attaching to such rituals requires a considerable effort of imagination. Again, the Prophets and others condemned idolatry. But what forms did this idolatry take? What were the kinds of non-Jewish and Canaanite religion which intermingled with and penetrated Jewish culture at various times? These questions again call on considerable factual and imaginative resources. What, again, were the Messianic expectations in the time of Jesus? Without a grasp of what Jesus rejected, we can hardly appreciate fully what he claimed to be. The problems raised by the need to add a religious dimension to the imaginative reconstruction of Biblical history are thus considerable. Fortunately, they can be rendered easier of solution by the third principle mentioned earlier, to which we can now turn, namely the principle of progressive understanding.

It has been a theme of this book that religious ideas incorporate, among other things, a poetical element. This is one aspect of the way in which the overt sense of religious language often conceals deeper layers of meaning. Nowhere is this more obvious than in the parables of Jesus (so much so that we are uncertain in some cases what their "real point" is). This ambiguity between the overt and the deeper meanings is the source of many religious or quasi-religious jokes (those about St Peter at the gates of heaven, for instance—though no one takes them seriously as a representation of a possible state of affairs). The process of understanding, therefore, involves a progression from the literal and overt to the poetical and analogical meaning concealed and yet also revealed through the literal. This seems to be a necessary feature of religious learning.

If so, it implies something important about the mode of teaching. This something I call the principle of progressive understanding. Clearly the deeper, more "advanced" understanding, cannot come about until first the stories and hymns and parables have been assimilated at a more "primitive" level. It follows that the straight presentation of portions of the Biblical material to children at a younger age is a necessary part of the progression to a more sensitive and informed understanding. The danger is that this may remain a stage beyond which the child is not taken. But by recognition of the principle that understanding should be and necessarily is progressive, if it is to penetrate to the heart of the matter, this danger can be overcome. The principle of progressive understanding implies a continual sifting and winnowing of the material—a continual attempt to apply the dialectic between revelation and experience at deeper and deeper levels. This implies something about the so-called "gap" discussed at the outset of this chapter.

Theological and philosophical reflection on Christian belief may never reach the end-point of understanding the full meaning of that belief. But it is nearer that end-point than is the situation of the child first learning about religion. The teacher cannot effectively draw on the child through the stages of progression towards fuller understanding unless he is himself already quite far along the path. The "gap" is thus a necessary feature of the situation, imposed by the principle of progressive understanding.

It is worth noting too that it is of the essence of progression that there be a revision of former understanding. That is, insight into religious belief itself is revisionary. A literal interpretation here, a naïve acceptance there, a misunderstanding of history in another place—these necessarily have to be discarded in the progressive framing of a more comprehensive, rational and sensitive picture of what the Biblical material points us to.

The principle of progressive understanding, we suggested a little earlier, can help to solve the problem of using our historical imagination to get back to the religious ideas (such as those clustering round ritual sacrifice) of Biblical times. How is this so? The answer is, roughly, as follows. We can be brought up to read the Old Testament in an accepting, rather literal way. We simply take its events and its ideas (not that we yet know fully what they really signify) for granted. At this level, the Old Testament narrative is "natural". It is unquestioned. This early stage of acceptance not only gives us an acquaintance with the text—with the stuff of the narrative—, but it also may, at an unconscious level, give us some of the feel of the sentiments and motives underlying the institutions and rituals of these ancient times. Then, when a critical awareness is aroused, and when we first begin to exercise historical imagination, we begin to look at all these old things afresh. We can come to ask: and what sort of thing really was this form of sacrifice. We can ask: what did these men hope to express and to gain by these ceremonials? The familiar takes on a strange appearance. Though we have not lived through the evolution of Old Testament religion, we have done something analogous to that historical experience. We have broken free from treating the familiar as familiar. We are on the move towards new insights. We have risen from acceptance to a critical reappraisal of what we have accepted. This is an analogy to the very process whereby the Prophets came to reinterpret and deepen the religion of their environment. In short, the process of progressive understanding can be a kind of recapitulation of the Biblical story itself.

Yet actually, and ultimately, the recapitulation of the Biblical experience must go much further, for the dialectic between our own experience and revelation must incorporate the history of the Church and the history of human thought in general down to the present day. That is, revelation is heir to the doctrines hammered out in the course of the Church's history; while modern experience is heir to the scientific, social, artistic and other developments which have helped to create the contemporary world. Thus the recapitulation, once it reaches a full philosophical and theological level, extends down to the present day. What we need, then, in education is a means of telescoping, for the individual, these long and exciting processes of interplay between revelation and its human environment. The principle of progressive understanding is thus more than a tactic. It is an expression of what we aim at throughout education, in seeking to make the individual an heir to a tradition which has taken generations to shape—whether that tradition be the history of modern physics, the literature of the ancient world or the appreciation of music.

These remarks serve to suggest a deeper way in which the three principles which we have enunciated (the dialectical principle and the principles of historical realism and of progressive understanding) are a consequence of theological and philosophical reflection. So far, all that can be said is that the principles chime in with a certain line of approach to the problems raised by the confrontation of Christian belief with the world of modern knowledge and experience. So far it is just a matter of a coincidence of methods. But there is another level at which the three principles flow from theology.

Consider first the dialectical principle—that teaching and learning must involve here an interplay between revelation and modern knowledge. This principle only reflects the more general fact that the world (according to Christian belief) incorporates a dialectic between God's creative and revealing work. God has made the whole world; has conferred the powers of reasoning, insight and love upon men; and has thereby made possible the increasing awareness and control through which men can understand and direct their environment. The arts, science, historical methods, complex forms of social organisation, technology, moral compassion, the sense of justice—all these arise out of the interplay between men and their environment, both sides of this interplay being created and sustained by God. Thus modern knowledge (from the Christian point of view) is itself one side of God's activity as Creator and as the Spirit of truth. The other side of the dialectic—God's revelation in history —is even more obviously to be ascribed to divine action. Thus the world itself displays a dialectical interplay between divine forces. In making use of the dialectical principle in education, we are only reflecting this general fact. Consequently, the dialectical principle has a theological, as well as a practical, significance.

Consider next the principle of historical realism. According to Christian doctrine, it needs no stressing, God has revealed himself in history. But history is not an abstract of facts which we consult in text-books. It is comprised of the interacting lives of men and their environment. Men are men, not myths. Thus it is intrinsic to the Christian conception of revelation that we should not be content with the Christ of religious experience, but must appreciate in as full a detail as is open to us the human Jesus who lived and died in Palestine. When bitten by flies, he would scratch himself: he is not just the person transfigured on Mount Tabor or beautifully and powerfully represented in icons. The transfiguration and the icons remain important; but they must not blind us to the human reality lying behind them. If this is so, a realistic investigation of the history of Jesus (and behind that the history of Israel) is a necessary consequence of the doctrine of the Incarnation. It is one of the great merits of modern Christianity that it is so historically self-critical, so realistic, so little inclined to be fobbed off by speculations. Thus the principle of historical realism, like the dialectical principle, is not merely a method: it is an intrinsic part of the Christian attitude.

Thirdly, the principle of progressive understanding is in line with the findings of theology, precisely because it involves a recapitulation of the history of Israel and of the Church, in the search for, and the acqusition of, a deeper understanding of the actions and nature of God. As we have seen in an earlier chapter, history has a certain "directionality". This need not be equated with unmitigated progress. Very often, this evolutionary vision breaks down. Nevertheless, the directionality of revealed history implies some kind of (albeit jerky) progress—the revision of earlier judgments, the insight into new dimensions of faith, the novel arrival of new forces in God's unfolding purpose. Thus the idea of recapitulating this process through the application of the principle of progressive understanding mirrors the Christian's need to assimilate the historical revelation in Israel and in the Church into his own personal experience. Once again, what at one level is an educational principle is at another level a consequence of Christian belief.

The three guiding principles enunciated here need, however, to be seen in still another perspective. It is intrinsic to the idea of contemporary knowledge and experience that these are in an important way *independent* of what is given in revelation. Though it may be the case that they can be illumined by revelation, and can themselves illuminate revelation, so that through this interplay the Christian can acquire a synthesis between the two, nevertheless, each side of the polarity is autonomous. This means that the educationist cannot regard religious knowledge, however much it may incorporate the findings of modern knowledge and the feel of contemporary experience, as an independent subject. It is a subject which is necessarily related to other subjects of teaching. The historical realism with which the Bible is treated does not differ in essential character from the historical realism with which we must approach Napoleon. The progressive understanding does not differ in principle from that which is employed in the study of literature. The dialectic does not differ in kind from the interplay between art appreciation and history. Thus the rigorous requirements of specialisation must not stand in the way of a relation between subjects at the academic level.

The ultimate answer, then, the main question posed in this chapter—the question of the relevance of theology—is that theological reflection itself is intimately bound up with the guiding principles through which theology itself must be taught. It is itself the source from which the methods flow. It is, moreover, at least a stage on the way towards a full understanding of revelation and its relation to the world, so that it is possible, from this higher stage, for Christian belief to act as a magnet to those whose knowledge is only commencing.

Yet it must not be forgotten in all this that we remain in a plural society. Neither all those who teach nor all those who learn will find Christian belief acceptable. But surely the main aim of the teaching of religion should be to exhibit the relevance of religious faith and action, both to the human past and to the human present. This relevance can best be shown by a reflective attempt at incorporating into the teaching of the Biblical and other material a theological perspective which takes into its purview both the religious tradition and the state of contemporary knowledge and experience. That is, though religion may in the long run strike some as false, it should at least be taught in such a way that it is acknowledged to be relevant. Likewise, we may reject Marxism without denying its relevance. It is thus in the interests both of the serious humanist and of the Christian that a relevant and reflective form of Christian belief be presented to those whose commitments and insights are in the process of formation.

It is therefore possible to see an inner unity in the trinity of guiding principles which have here been enunciated. The unity consists in this: that the teaching of religion itself cannot function unless already there is an informed and reflective point of view from which the teaching flows. To put the matter differently: theology itself is the inner unity of these three principles.

We may thus answer the question: Is theology relevant? by the answer: Theology is relevant, if it is relevant theology. It can be so by being dialectical, historically realistic and progressive. These, however, are hard demands, for they require broadness of education, a powerful equipment of linguistic and historical skills and a readiness to be revisionary. It is only through the community of scholars, perhaps, rather than through the efforts of a single person, that such a theology can be attained. This is an added reason why the discussions of the present book should be thought of as a cockshy only. It is also a reason why the teaching of religion, in all its manifestations, should not be compartmentalised. Only thus can it take its proper place in the work of forming the new society.

In substance, then, the teaching of religion must reflect the structure of the world which Christian belief tries to illuminate, and its methods and content should be in a state of solidarity. Perhaps the solidarity for which I have argued is not the correct one. This is of no great importance, provided that some coherent alternative is put in its place. There must be many such alternatives. It *is* important, though, that we search.

BIBLIOGRAPHY

WHERE a book is relevant to a particular paragraph, the number of that paragraph is placed after the page number. For example, 81/1 refers to the first paragraph on page 81 (i.e. the first paragraph which actually begins on page 81, and excluding part of a paragraph begun on page 80).

11   F. H. Hilliard, *The Teacher and Religion* (1963), especially chapter 5.

13/1   See the essay "A Critique of Humanist Theology" by Ronald Hepburn in *Objections to Humanism*, ed. H. J. Blackham (Pelican edition, 1965).

17ff.   John Baillie, *The Idea of Revelation in Recent Thought* (1956).

22/2   Karl Barth, *Dogmatics in Outline*, tr. G. T. Thomson (1959); also John Macquarrie, *Twentieth Century Religious Thought* (1963), §95.

22/3   Macquarrie (see 22/2), §82 (Temple); ch. xviii (*Roman Catholic Theology*): §107 (Bultmann), and see H. P. Owen, *Revelation and Existence* (1957); H. D. Macdonald, *Theories of Revelation* (1963) (the Conservative Evangelical viewpoint).

26/1   Austin Farrer, *The Glass of Vision* (1948).

27/3   Macquarrie (see 22/2), ch. xv.

36ff.   Karl Popper, *Conjectures and Refutations* (1963); Rom Harré, *Theories and Things* (1961) and *Matter and Method* (1965); Arthur Koestler, *The Sleep-Walkers* (1959).

36/4   Bertrand Russell, *My Philosophical Development* (1959); A. J. Ayer, *Language Truth and Logic* (2nd edn., 1946); Macquarrie (see 22/2), §92.

41/2   David Lack, *Evolutionary Theory and Christian Belief* (1959).

44ff.   Ninian Smart, *Philosophers and Religious Truth* (1964), ch. ii.

47/1   K. Popper, *Conjectures and Refutations* (1963).

54/1   N. Smart, *Historical Selections in the Philosophy of Religion*, ch. 5 §A; ch. 13 §A; ch. 14 §A.

59/1   David E. Roberts, *Existentialism and Religious Belief* (1957).

59/2   H. Bondi and others, *Rival Theories of Cosmology* (1956).

69ff.   Frederic Greeves, *The Meaning of Sin* (1956).

74/3   Gustav Aulén, *Christus Victor*, tr. A. G. Hebert (1953).

79/2   Smart (see 54/1), ch. 4 §B; Alan Montefiore, *A Modern Introduction to Moral Philosophy* (1958). ch. 4; Austin Farrer, *Freedom of the Will* (1958).

82/2   Patrick Nowell-Smith, *Ethics* (1954), ch. 20.

85/1   Ninian Smart, *Philosophers and Religious Truth* (1964), ch. iii.

97/1   Teilhard de Chardin, *The Phenomenon of Man* (1959).

102ff. Ninian Smart, *A Dialogue of Religions* (1960); R. C. Zaehner (ed.), *Concise Encyclopedia of Living Faiths* (1959).

105/1   John Yale (ed.), *What Vedānta means to me* (1959).

109/2   R. C. Zaehner, *At Sundry Times* (1958).

110/1   Ninian Smart, *Doctrine and Argument in Indian Philosophy* (1964), ch. x.

115/1   Sarvepalli Radhakrishnan, *The Hindu View of Life* (1927).

128/2   S. Radhakrishnan, *The Bhagavadgītā* (1949).

141ff.   A. C. Ewing, *Teach Yourself Ethics* (1953).

144/3   John Stuart Mill, *Utilitarianism*, ed. J. P. Plamenatz (1949).

146/2   H. J. Paton, *The Categorical Imperative* (2nd edn., 1953).

160/1   Karl Popper, *The Poverty of Historicism* (1957).

172ff.   R. S. Franks, *The Doctrine of the Trinity* (1953).

INDEX

Abraham, 58, 137
Aquinas, St. Thomas, 22, 54
Aristotle, 61
Arjuna, 128
Arthur, King, 33
Ayer, A. J., 36, 37, 46

Barth, Karl, 22
Boehme, Jakob, 107, 113
Brahms, Johannes, 164
Buddha, the, 14, 110, 113, 129, 137, 139
Bultmann, Rudolf, 9

Calvin, Jean, 113

Darwin, Charles, 21, 41, 42, 120
Dostoievsky, Fyodor, 161

Eckhart, Meister, 107, 113
Einstein, Alfred, 48, 86

Freud, Sigmund, 130, 131, 183

Galileo, 41
Gamow, George, 60
Gandhi, M. K., 183

Hoyle, Fred, 60
Hume, David, 54
Huxley, T. H., 41

Isaiah, 128

Jeremiah, 169
Jesus, 14, 21, 34, 46, 65, 74, 75, 79, 123, 175, 176, 177, 192, 193, 194, 195
John of the Cross, St., 107, 110, 113
Johnson, Lyndon B., 93, 174
Jonah, 21

Kant, Immanuel, 54, 79, 146, 147
Knox, John, 113

Mill, John Stuart, 144
Mozart, Wolfgang Amadeus, 164
Muhammad, 113, 130

Napoleon, 33
Newton, Isaac, 48

Paul, St., 20, 78, 91, 134
Peter, St., 10
Pilate, Pontius, 183
Popper, Karl, 36, 50

Ramanuja, 105
Robinson, John, 27, 28, 186
Russell, Bertrand, 36, 38

Sartre, Jean-Paul, 59
Shakespeare, William, 87
Shankara, 98
Socrates, 74, 188